Dedication

To my beloved parents,

You nurtured my dreams from the seeds of imagination to the blossoms of reality. Your love, sacrifice, and unwavering belief in me have been my constant source of strength and inspiration. This book is a tribute to your endless support and the home you've always provided for my aspirations.

To my dearest spouse,

You have been my rock, my sanctuary, and my biggest cheerleader. In the labyrinth of life, your love and support have been my guiding star. This book mirrors our journey together – filled with love, resilience, and shared dreams.

And to my wonderful children,

You are the joy and light of my life. Watching you grow and explore the world with wide-eyed wonder has rekindled my own sense of curiosity and adventure. This book is not just a product of my imagination, but also of the countless stories and dreams we've shared. May it remind you always to chase your dreams, as you have inspired me to chase mine.

With all my love and gratitude,

Sandeep Kumar Pandey

Table of Contents

Chapter 1: Introduction to Data Engineering

- Understanding the Role of Data Engineers
- The Data Engineering Ecosystem
- Data Quality Fundamentals
- Hands-On: Setting Up **ADLS** with Python

Chapter 2: Data Modeling and Database Design

- The Fundamentals of Data Modeling
- Normalization and Denormalization
- Database Design Best Practices
- Hands-On: Using **Azure Synapse Analytics** to create a relational data warehouse.

Chapter 3: Extract, Transform, Load (ETL)

- Exploring the ETL Lifecycle
- ETL Tools and Technologies
- Building Effective ETL Pipelines
- Hands-On: Building a complete ETL pipeline using **ADF** and **Databricks**.

Chapter 4: Data Warehousing

- Introduction to Data Warehouses
- Data Warehousing Architecture and Solutions
- Hands-On: Build a star-schema data warehouse in **Azure Synapse** and load data using **Python**.

Chapter 5: Data Integration and Ingestion

- Strategies for Data Integration
- Real-time Data Integration with Streaming
- Hands-On: Stream data from external APIs into Azure Synapse using Databricks Spark Streaming.

Chapter 6: Data Quality and Data Governance

- Ensuring Data Quality
- Data Governance Principles and Best Practices
- Data Lineage and Data Catalogs
- Hands-On: Implement data quality checks with **Python** and monitor data lineage using **Azure Purview**.

Chapter 7: Data Pipeline Optimization

- Optimizing Data Processing Pipelines

- Scalability and Performance Tuning
- Monitoring and Troubleshooting
- Hands-On: Optimize an existing ETL pipeline using **Databricks** and **ADF**, and set up monitoring to track pipeline performance.

Chapter 8: Data Security and Compliance

- Data Security Best Practices
- Compliance and Regulatory Requirements
- Data Encryption and Access Control
- Hands-On: Configure RBAC and encryption in Azure to secure your data lake and warehouse.

Chapter 9: Real-World Case Studies

- **Case Study 1**: Building a Scalable Data Pipeline
  Build a real-world scalable pipeline using ADLS, ADF, and Azure Synapse to process millions of rows of data.
- **Case Study 2**: Data Quality Assurance in Practice
  Implement a quality assurance system in Databricks to validate data in a business-critical pipeline.
- **Practical Example**: Use all concepts learned in previous chapters to design, build, and optimize a full data pipeline for a business intelligence use case.

Introduction to Data Engineering: A Practical Approach

In the era of big data and advanced analytics, **Data Engineering** has become a critical function in modern organizations. It provides the foundation upon which data-driven decision-making is built, ensuring that data is reliable, accessible, and usable for analytics, machine learning, and business intelligence. This book, "**Data Engineering: A Practical Approach**," is designed to equip aspiring data engineers and professionals with the essential skills and knowledge to build and optimize data pipelines, manage large datasets, and implement scalable data solutions using cutting-edge tools and cloud services like **Azure**.

Who is this book for?

This book is tailored for readers from a **software engineering background**—whether you are an engineering student looking to expand your knowledge or a working professional with little or no experience in data engineering, but eager to enhance your skills. Even if you have a foundational understanding of data engineering, this book provides **deep-dive explanations** and **practical examples** to help you master advanced topics.

We focus on **theory and hands-on practice** using **Python** and **Azure services**, including **Azure Data Lake Storage (ADLS)**, **Azure Data Factory (ADF)**, **Azure Synapse Analytics**, **Azure Databricks**, and **Azure Machine Learning (AML)**. These cloud services are industry-standard tools for building scalable, efficient, and reliable data pipelines and architectures.

Why is this book different?

This book doesn't just introduce you to concepts—it provides **real-world, actionable knowledge**. From the very first chapter, you will work hands-on with practical examples and exercises. By the end of this book, you will have built and optimized multiple data pipelines, learned how to manage large-scale data warehouses, and gained experience with state-of-the-art tools used by data engineers in the industry.

What tools and technologies will you use?

Throughout the book, you will work with industry-leading tools and cloud services, including:

- **Python**: A versatile programming language widely used for data engineering and ETL.
- **Azure Data Lake Storage (ADLS)**: Scalable storage for unstructured data.
- **Azure Data Factory (ADF)**: A cloud-based ETL tool for orchestrating data pipelines.
- **Azure Synapse Analytics**: A powerful analytics service that combines big data and data warehousing.
- **Azure Databricks**: A unified analytics platform built on Apache Spark for scalable data processing.
- **Azure Purview**: A data governance solution that helps track data lineage and catalog datasets.

Chapter 1: Introduction to Data Engineering

Data engineering follows a structured lifecycle, which includes several key phases:

The Data Engineering Lifecycle

1. **Data Ingestion**: In this phase, data engineers collect data from various sources and bring it into the data ecosystem.

2. **Data Transformation**: Data is cleaned, transformed, and enriched to ensure it's ready for analysis.

3. **Data Storage**: Transformed data is stored in data warehouses or data lakes.

4. **Data Access and Consumption**: Once data is stored, it becomes accessible for various purposes, including reporting, analysis, and application development.

5. **Monitoring and Maintenance**: Data pipelines and storage systems require continuous monitoring and maintenance to ensure they perform optimally.

6. **Data Governance**: Data governance practices ensure that data is used ethically, securely, and in compliance with regulations.

7. **Data Quality Assurance**: Maintaining data quality is an ongoing process that involves validation, error handling, and data profiling.

1.1 Understanding the Role of Data Engineering

Data engineering is the backbone of modern data-driven organizations. The role of data engineers is to ensure that data is accessible, reliable, and usable for data scientists, analysts, and business stakeholders. They design, build, and manage scalable data pipelines that transform raw data into meaningful insights.

1.1.1 What is Data Engineering?

Data engineering involves developing systems that collect, store, and analyze data at scale. The goal is to ensure that data flows smoothly from its source to its destination, where it can be used for analytics, reporting, and machine learning.

Key Responsibilities:

- Design and build data pipelines.
- Maintain data warehouses and lakes.
- Ensure data quality and integrity.
- Automate data workflows and processes.

1.1.2 Importance in the Modern Data Landscape

In a world driven by data, data engineers ensure that data is available in the right form and at the right time. Companies like

5. **Monitoring and Maintenance**: Data pipelines and storage systems require continuous monitoring and maintenance to ensure they perform optimally.

6. **Data Governance**: Data governance practices ensure that data is used ethically, securely, and in compliance with regulations.

7. **Data Quality Assurance**: Maintaining data quality is an ongoing process that involves validation, error handling, and data profiling.

1.1 Understanding the Role of Data Engineering

Data engineering is the backbone of modern data-driven organizations. The role of data engineers is to ensure that data is accessible, reliable, and usable for data scientists, analysts, and business stakeholders. They design, build, and manage scalable data pipelines that transform raw data into meaningful insights.

1.1.1 What is Data Engineering?

Data engineering involves developing systems that collect, store, and analyze data at scale. The goal is to ensure that data flows smoothly from its source to its destination, where it can be used for analytics, reporting, and machine learning.

Key Responsibilities:

- Design and build data pipelines.
- Maintain data warehouses and lakes.
- Ensure data quality and integrity.
- Automate data workflows and processes.

1.1.2 Importance in the Modern Data Landscape

In a world driven by data, data engineers ensure that data is available in the right form and at the right time. Companies like

Amazon, Netflix, and Facebook rely heavily on data engineers to keep their data systems operational and efficient.

Why is Data Engineering Critical?

- Supports business intelligence and decision-making.
- Enables machine learning and AI workflows.
- Handles large volumes of data generated by modern applications.

1.1.3 Career Pathways and Opportunities

Data engineering is a growing field with numerous opportunities. With skills in cloud platforms like Azure, programming in Python, and knowledge of data frameworks like Spark and Hadoop, data engineers are in high demand.

Skills Required:

- Proficiency in Python, SQL, and data manipulation libraries.

- Knowledge of cloud services (Azure, AWS, GCP).
- Understanding of database systems (SQL and NoSQL).
- Familiarity with big data tools (Hadoop, Spark).

1.1.4 Practical Example: Setting Up a Data Engineering Environment

Let's start by setting up your Python and Azure environment, which will be used throughout this book.

Step 1: Install Python and Required Libraries

1. Install Python from python.org.
2. Install essential libraries using pip:

```
pip install pandas pyarrow azure-storage-blob
```

Step 2: Set Up Azure Data Lake Storage (ADLS)

Azure Data Lake Storage (ADLS) is used for scalable data storage. To set it up:

1. Go to the Azure Portal.
2. Create a new **Storage Account** and enable **Hierarchical namespace** to use ADLS Gen2.
3. Note down the storage account name and access keys for later use.

Step 3: Connecting Python to ADLS

Use the Azure SDK for Python to interact with your storage account. Here's how to connect and upload a file:

```
# Define your connection string
connection_string = "DefaultEndpointsProtocol=https;AccountName=<your_account_name

# Create the BlobServiceClient object
blob_service_client = BlobServiceClient.from_connection_string(connection_string)

# Create a container in your storage account
container_name = 'test-container'
container_client = blob_service_client.get_container_client(container_name)
container_client.create_container()

# Upload a file to the container
blob_client = container_client.get_blob_client("sample.txt")
with open("sample.txt", "rb") as data:
    blob_client.upload_blob(data)
```

This Python script will create a container and upload a text file to your Azure Data Lake.

1.2 The Data Engineering Ecosystem

The data engineering ecosystem is vast, comprising various tools, frameworks, and services that enable the processing, storage, and analysis of data. In this section, we will explore these components.

1.2.1 Core Components

1. **Data Sources:** Data comes from various sources such as databases, APIs, and streaming platforms.
2. **Data Storage:** Azure Data Lake (for unstructured data) and Azure Synapse Analytics (for structured data).
3. **Data Processing:** Frameworks like Apache Spark allow for scalable data transformations.

1.2.2 Tools and Technologies

- **Azure Data Factory (ADF):** A cloud-based ETL service for orchestrating data workflows.
- **Databricks:** A platform that provides an integrated environment for running Spark workloads.
- **Python Libraries:** Pandas for data manipulation, PySpark for distributed processing.

1.2.3 Practical Example: Exploring Azure Services

Let's create an Azure Data Factory instance and connect it to Python.

Step 1: Create Azure Data Factory (ADF)

1. Go to the Azure Portal.
2. Search for **Data Factory** and create a new instance.
3. Name your instance and select a region.

Step 2: Navigating Azure Portal

Once your ADF is set up, you can create data pipelines that connect to various data sources, including ADLS, SQL databases, and APIs.

Step 3: Using Python to Connect to ADF

You can connect to ADF using Python SDKs to automate ETL tasks.

```
from azure.identity import DefaultAzureCredential
from azure.mgmt.datafactory import DataFactoryManagementClient

# Get credentials
credentials = DefaultAzureCredential()

# Initialize ADF client
adf_client = DataFactoryManagementClient(credentials, '<your_subscription_id>')

# Check for the ADF instance
factory = adf_client.factories.get('<your_resource_group>', '<your_adf_name>')
print(factory.name)
```

1.3 The Importance of Data Quality

Data quality is one of the most critical aspects of data engineering. Poor quality data leads to incorrect insights and bad decision-making. In this section, we will focus on the dimensions of data quality and practical ways to ensure it.

1.3.1 Dimensions of Data Quality

1. **Accuracy:** Ensuring that the data reflects real-world entities correctly.
2. **Completeness:** Making sure all required data is available.
3. **Consistency:** Data should be uniform across datasets.
4. **Timeliness:** Data should be up-to-date and available when needed.

1.3.2 Practical Example: Data Quality Checks

In this example, we will use Python to check for missing values and data inconsistencies in a dataset stored in Azure Data Lake.

Step 1: Read Data from ADLS

```python
import pandas as pd
from azure.storage.blob import BlobServiceClient

# Connect to ADLS
blob_service_client = BlobServiceClient.from_connection_string(connection_string)
container_client = blob_service_client.get_container_client('data-container')

# Download a CSV file from the data lake
blob_client = container_client.get_blob_client('data.csv')
stream_downloader = blob_client.download_blob()
data = pd.read_csv(stream_downloader.readall())

# Display the first few rows
print(data.head())
```

Step 2: Perform Data Quality Checks

- Check for Missing Values:

```python
missing_values = data.isnull().sum()
print("Missing values:\n", missing_values)
```

- Check for Duplicate Records:

```python
duplicates = data[data.duplicated()]
print(f"Number of duplicate records: {duplicates.shape[0]}")
```

Step 3: Logging Data Quality Issues

Log any issues found during the data quality checks.

```
with open('data_quality_log.txt', 'w') as log_file:
    log_file.write(f"Missing values:\n{missing_values}\n")
    log_file.write(f"Duplicate records: {duplicates.shape[0]}\n")

# Upload the log back to ADLS
blob_client = container_client.get_blob_client('data_quality_log.txt')
with open('data_quality_log.txt', 'rb') as log_data:
    blob_client.upload_blob(log_data, overwrite=True)
```

1.4 Setting the Stage for Practical Data Engineering

In this section, we'll explore a real-world data engineering scenario. You will build a data pipeline that ingests customer transaction data from an e-commerce platform, processes it for analysis, and stores it in a data warehouse for business insights.

1.4.1 Sample Project: E-Commerce Data Pipeline

- **Data Sources:** Customer orders, transaction logs, web activity.
- **Data Storage:** Raw data in **Azure Data Lake**, processed data in **Azure Synapse Analytics**.
- **Data Processing:** Using **Databricks** to clean, transform, and load data.

1.4.2 Practical Example: Data Ingestion Script

Here's how to create a simple Python script to ingest data into Azure Data Lake.

```python
# Sample data for ingestion
data = {
    'customer_id': [101, 102, 103],
    'order_id': [1, 2, 3],
    'order_amount': [250.75, 300.50, 100.25]
}

# Convert to DataFrame
df = pd.DataFrame(data)

# Save to CSV and upload to ADLS
df.to_csv('orders.csv', index=False)

blob_client = container_client.get_blob_client('orders.csv')
with open('orders.csv', 'rb') as file_data:
    blob_client.upload_blob(file_data, overwrite=True)
```

1.5 Summary and Next Steps

In this chapter, you learned:

- The key role data engineers play in managing and processing data.
- The tools and technologies that make up the data engineering ecosystem.

- How to set up a development environment using Python and Azure services.

In the next chapter, we'll dive into **Data Modeling and Database Design**, where you'll learn how to structure and organize your data for efficient querying and analysis.

Hands-on Assignment:

- Set up your Azure account and explore **Azure Data Lake**.
- Write a Python script to upload data to your ADLS.
- Perform data quality checks on a sample dataset and document any issues.

Chapter 2: Data Modeling and Database Design

In the previous chapter, we explored the foundational concepts of data engineering, its role in the modern data-driven landscape, and the essential components of the data engineering ecosystem. Now, we turn our attention to a critical aspect of data engineering: data modeling and database design. These concepts are the building blocks upon which data engineering processes are constructed. In this chapter, we will delve into the intricacies of data modeling, the principles of database design, and best practices for structuring data to ensure its integrity, efficiency, and usability.

The Significance of Data Modeling

Data modeling is the process of defining the structure and relationships of data to represent a specific domain of interest. It is a fundamental step in the data engineering process as it lays the foundation for how data will be organized and stored within databases. Effective data modeling is crucial for the following reasons:

1. **Structural Clarity**: Data modeling provides a clear and systematic representation of data entities, their attributes, and their relationships. This clarity facilitates understanding, communication, and collaboration among data engineers, stakeholders, and other team members.
2. **Efficiency**: Well-designed data models lead to efficient data storage and retrieval. Properly structured data reduces redundancy and minimizes the amount of

storage space required. It also speeds up data access and query performance.

3. **Data Integrity**: Data modeling enforces rules and constraints to maintain data integrity. By specifying data types, relationships, and validation rules, data models help ensure that data remains accurate and consistent over time.
4. **Scalability**: A good data model accommodates growth and changes in data volume and complexity. It provides a flexible structure that can adapt to evolving business needs without major disruptions.

The Components of Data Modeling

Data modeling involves several key components:

1. **Entities**: Entities represent objects or concepts in the real world, such as customers, products, or orders. They serve as the primary building blocks of a data model.
2. **Attributes**: Attributes are the properties or characteristics of entities. For example, a "Customer" entity might have attributes like "Name," "Address," and "Email."
3. **Relationships**: Relationships describe the connections or associations between entities. They reveal how different entities are related to each other. Relationships can be one-to-one, one-to-many, or many-to-many.
4. **Keys**: Keys are attributes that uniquely identify each instance of an entity.
   A primary key is the main identifier, and there can be alternate keys as well.

5. **Constraints**: Constraints define rules and conditions that must be met for data to be valid. Examples include uniqueness constraints, referential integrity constraints, and data type constraints.

Types of Data Models

There are various types of data models used in data engineering, each serving specific purposes. The choice of a data model depends on the nature of the data and the requirements of the application. Here are some common data model types:

1. **Conceptual Data Model**: This high-level model provides an abstract representation of the data and its relationships. It focuses on the entities and their associations without delving into technical implementation details.
2. **Logical Data Model**: The logical data model describes the structure of the data in a technology-agnostic manner. It specifies entities, attributes, and relationships but does not concern itself with the specifics of database systems.
3. **Physical Data Model**: The physical data model is implementation-specific and details how the data will be stored in a particular database management system. It includes information about data types, indexes, and storage mechanisms.
4. **Relational Data Model**: The relational data model represents data using tables, where each table corresponds to an entity, and each row in the table represents an instance of that entity. Relationships between entities are defined through foreign keys.

5. **NoSQL Data Model**: NoSQL databases employ various data models, such as document, key-value, column-family, or graph, to accommodate different data structures and requirements. These models are designed to handle unstructured or semi-structured data.

Data Modeling Approaches

Data modeling can be approached using different methods, depending on the project's goals and requirements. Here are two common data modeling approaches:

1. **Entity-Relationship Diagrams (ERD)**: ERDs are graphical representations of entities, attributes, and their relationships. They use symbols like rectangles (entities), ovals (attributes), and lines (relationships) to visually depict the data model. ERDs are widely used for conceptual and logical data modeling.
2. **UML (Unified Modeling Language)**: UML is a general-purpose modeling language that can be used for various types of modeling, including data modeling. UML diagrams, such as class diagrams, can represent data structures and their relationships.

Normalization and Denormalization

Normalization is a process in which data is organized in a database to reduce redundancy and improve data integrity. It involves breaking down data into smaller, related tables to eliminate data duplication. Normalization follows a set of rules (called normal forms) to ensure that data is stored efficiently and without anomalies. The goal is to minimize data redundancy and ensure that each fact is stored in only one place.

For example, consider a database for a library. Instead of storing the same book details (e.g., title, author, and ISBN) for every copy of the book, normalization would involve creating a separate table for books and another for copies. The book details are stored in the book table, and the copy details (e.g., location and condition) are stored in the copy table. This minimizes redundancy and ensures consistency.

Denormalization, on the other hand, is the process of deliberately introducing redundancy into a database for the sake of improving query performance. While normalization is beneficial for data integrity, it can sometimes lead to complex joins and slower query performance. Denormalization can address these issues by storing related data in a single table. However, it's essential to strike a balance between normalization and denormalization based on the specific needs of the application.

Database Design Best Practices

Effective database design is essential for the performance and scalability of data systems. Here are some best practices for designing databases:

1. **Understand the Requirements**: Begin by thoroughly understanding the requirements of the application. What data needs to be stored? How will it be accessed and queried? This understanding guides the design process.

2. **Choose the Right Data Model**: Select the appropriate data model for your application. For structured, tabular data, a relational database may be suitable, while unstructured or semi-structured data may require a NoSQL database.
3. **Design for Data Integrity**: Enforce data integrity through constraints and validations. Define primary keys, foreign keys, and constraints to ensure data consistency.
4. **Optimize for Query Performance**: Consider the types of queries that will be executed on the database. Create appropriate indexes to speed up query performance.
5. **Consider Scalability**: Design your database with scalability in mind. Be prepared for data growth and evolving requirements.
6. **Document Your Design**: Thoroughly document your database design, including entity-relationship diagrams, constraints, and any denormalization choices. This documentation is invaluable for maintenance and future development.
7. **Test and Refine**: Before deploying your database, test it with sample data and real-world scenarios. Identify and address any performance bottlenecks or issues.
8. **Backup and Recovery**: Implement robust backup and recovery procedures to safeguard your data in case of data loss or system failures.

Case Study: Database Design for an E-commerce Platform

To illustrate the principles of data modeling and database design, let's consider a case study for an e-commerce platform. This platform needs to store data about customers, products, orders, and payments. Here's a simplified example of how the data model might look:

- **Entities**:
    - Customer
    - Product
    - Order
    - Payment
- **Attributes**:
    - Customer: customer_id, name, email, address
    - Product: product_id, name, description, price
    - Order: order_id, customer_id, order_date
    - Payment: payment_id, order_id, amount, payment_date
- **Relationships**:
    - A Customer can place multiple Orders.
    - An Order can include multiple Products.
    - Each Order is associated with one Payment.
- **Keys**:
    - Customer: customer_id (primary key)
    - Product: product_id (primary key)
    - Order: order_id (primary key), customer_id (foreign key)
    - Payment: payment_id (primary key), order_id (foreign key)

This data model provides a structured representation of the e-commerce platform's data, specifying entities, attributes, relationships, and keys. It can serve as the basis for creating a database that stores and manages data for the platform.

Practical Example: Using Azure Synapse to Create and Manage a Relational Data Warehouse

In this practical example, we will create a relational data warehouse in **Azure Synapse Analytics**, design its schema, and implement normalization principles. Azure Synapse is a powerful cloud-based service that combines big data and data warehousing, enabling us to process and analyze large amounts of structured data.

Objective:

By the end of this example, you will:

1. Understand how to create a relational data warehouse in Azure Synapse.
2. Learn about schema design and normalization principles.
3. Design and implement a 3NF-compliant schema.
4. Load and query data in Azure Synapse using SQL.

Step-by-Step Walkthrough

Step 1: Set Up Azure Synapse Workspace

1. **Create a Synapse Workspace**
   - Go to the Azure Portal.

- Search for **Azure Synapse Analytics** and create a new workspace.
- Configure the workspace with a resource group, storage account, and network settings.
- Once the workspace is created, open **Synapse Studio** for data engineering and querying tasks.

2. **Create a Dedicated SQL Pool (Data Warehouse)**
   - In **Synapse Studio**, click on **Manage** > **SQL pools**.
   - Create a new **Dedicated SQL pool**. This will act as your data warehouse.
   - Name the pool (e.g., DataWarehousePool) and select the appropriate performance level based on your workload.

3. **Create a Database**
   - In Synapse Studio, go to **Data** > **Linked** > **Workspace SQL pools**.
   - Right-click on the **Dedicated SQL pool** and select **New SQL Script** > **Database**.
   - Execute the following query to create a database for your data warehouse:

```
CREATE DATABASE SalesDW;
```

Step 2: Schema Design and Normalization

In a relational data warehouse, schema design is crucial for ensuring efficient querying and storage. Normalization principles help in structuring data to reduce redundancy and improve data integrity.

2.1 Understanding Normalization

Normalization is the process of organizing data to minimize redundancy. The three common normal forms (3NF) include:

- **First Normal Form (1NF):** Eliminate duplicate columns and ensure atomic values in each column.
- **Second Normal Form (2NF):** Ensure that all non-key attributes depend on the primary key.
- **Third Normal Form (3NF):** Remove transitive dependencies (i.e., non-key attributes should only depend on the primary key).

In this practical example, we will design a **star schema** with normalized dimension tables and a denormalized fact table, suitable for analytical queries.

2.2 Designing a Schema for an E-commerce Sales Data Warehouse

Our data warehouse will track orders, customers, products, and sales.

- **Fact Table:**
  - SalesFact: Contains transactional data such as order ID, customer ID, product ID, quantity, price, and date.
- **Dimension Tables:**
  - CustomerDim: Contains information about customers such as customer ID, name, and region.
  - ProductDim: Contains product details such as product ID, name, category, and price.
  - DateDim: Stores date-related data such as day, month, and year.

Schema Diagram (Star Schema):

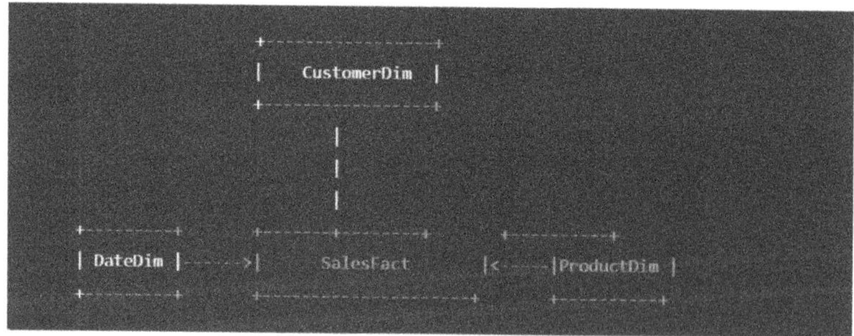

Step 3: Implementing the Schema in Azure Synapse

3.1 Creating Dimension Tables

We will begin by creating our normalized dimension tables. The **CustomerDim**, **ProductDim**, and **DateDim** tables will follow the 3NF guidelines.

Create Customer Dimension Table:

```
CREATE TABLE CustomerDim (
    CustomerID INT PRIMARY KEY,
    CustomerName VARCHAR(255),
    Region VARCHAR(100)
);
```

Create Product Dimension Table:

```
CREATE TABLE ProductDim (
    ProductID INT PRIMARY KEY,
    ProductName VARCHAR(255),
    Category VARCHAR(100),
    UnitPrice DECIMAL(10, 2)
);
```

Create Date Dimension Table:

```
CREATE TABLE DateDim (
    DateID INT PRIMARY KEY,
    Day INT,
    Month INT,
    Year INT
);
```

3.2 Creating Fact Table

The **SalesFact** table will be a denormalized fact table that references the dimension tables. It contains foreign keys to the dimension tables and stores the quantitative metrics of the transactions (e.g., quantity sold, total price).

Create Sales Fact Table:

```
CREATE TABLE SalesFact (
    SalesID INT PRIMARY KEY,
    CustomerID INT FOREIGN KEY REFERENCES CustomerDim(CustomerID),
    ProductID INT FOREIGN KEY REFERENCES ProductDim(ProductID),
    DateID INT FOREIGN KEY REFERENCES DateDim(DateID),
    Quantity INT,
    TotalPrice DECIMAL(10, 2)
);
```

Step 4: Loading Data into the Data Warehouse

We will now load data into the dimension and fact tables using SQL.

4.1 Insert Data into Dimension Tables

Insert Customers:

```sql
INSERT INTO CustomerDim (CustomerID, CustomerName, Region)
VALUES
(1, 'John Doe', 'North America'),
(2, 'Jane Smith', 'Europe');
```

Insert Products:

```sql
INSERT INTO ProductDim (ProductID, ProductName, Category, UnitPrice)
VALUES
(1, 'Laptop', 'Electronics', 1000.00),
(2, 'Smartphone', 'Electronics', 700.00);
```

Insert Dates:

```sql
INSERT INTO DateDim (DateID, Day, Month, Year)
VALUES
(1, 12, 9, 2023),
(2, 13, 9, 2023);
```

4.2 Insert Data into the Fact Table

Insert Sales Transactions:

```sql
INSERT INTO SalesFact (SalesID, CustomerID, ProductID, DateID, Quantity, TotalPrice)
VALUES
(1, 1, 1, 1, 2, 2000.00), -- John buys 2 Laptops
(2, 2, 2, 2, 1, 700.00);  -- Jane buys 1 Smartphone
```

Step 5: Querying the Data Warehouse

Once the data is loaded, we can query the data warehouse to analyze sales trends and generate insights.

Query: Calculate Total Sales by Region

```
SELECT c.Region, SUM(s.TotalPrice) AS TotalSales
FROM SalesFact s
JOIN CustomerDim c ON s.CustomerID = c.CustomerID
GROUP BY c.Region;
```

Query: Find Total Sales by Product Category

```
SELECT p.Category, SUM(s.TotalPrice) AS TotalSales
FROM SalesFact s
JOIN ProductDim p ON s.ProductID = p.ProductID
GROUP BY p.Category;
```

Step 6: Managing the Data Warehouse

6.1 Scaling and Monitoring

- **Performance Tuning:** Use **distribution** and **partitioning** in Azure Synapse to optimize performance for large datasets.

Example:

```
CREATE TABLE SalesFact
WITH (DISTRIBUTION = HASH(ProductID))  -- Use hash distribution for even distribution
AS
SELECT * FROM SalesFact;
```

- **Monitoring Queries:** Synapse provides query performance monitoring tools to analyze slow-running queries and optimize them.

6.2 Backup and Restore

Azure Synapse allows you to automate backups and restore points for your data warehouse.

- Go to **Manage** > **SQL pools** > **Backups** to configure automatic backups.

Conclusion

In this practical example, we walked through the process of setting up a relational data warehouse in **Azure Synapse**, designing a schema based on normalization principles, loading data into the data warehouse, and running queries to extract insights. We implemented a **star schema** architecture that balances data normalization in dimension tables and denormalization in the fact table, making it ideal for analytics workloads.

By following this example, you now have a fundamental understanding of how to design and manage data warehouses in Azure Synapse, a critical skill for data engineers working with large-scale data systems.

In the next chapters, we will continue to explore key concepts and practices in data engineering, delving into topics such as Extract, Transform, Load (ETL) processes, data warehousing, and data integration. These topics are critical for building the data pipelines and systems that enable data-driven decision-making and innovation.

Chapter 3: Extract, Transform, Load (ETL)

In the previous chapters, we explored the foundational concepts of data engineering, including the importance of data modeling and database design. We learned how data modeling forms the basis for organizing data within databases, ensuring data integrity, and enabling efficient data retrieval. Now, we turn our attention to one of the most critical phases of the data engineering process: Extract, Transform, Load (ETL).

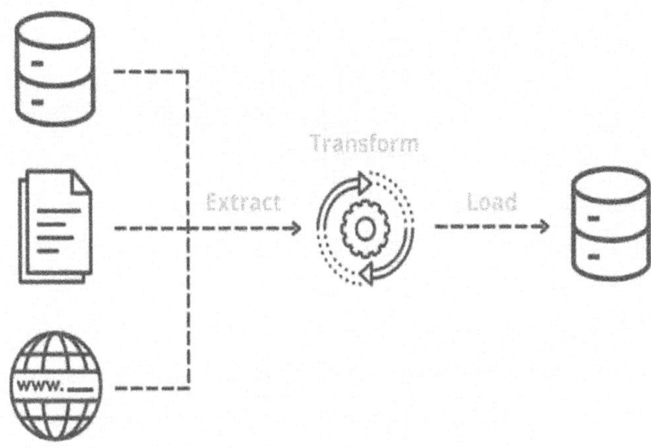

3.1 Exploring the ETL Lifecycle

ETL is the heart of data engineering, responsible for extracting data from various sources, transforming it into a suitable format, and loading it into a target system. In this chapter, we'll delve into the intricacies of ETL processes, understand its key components, explore the challenges, and examine best practices to create robust data pipelines.

Understanding ETL: Extract, Transform, and Load

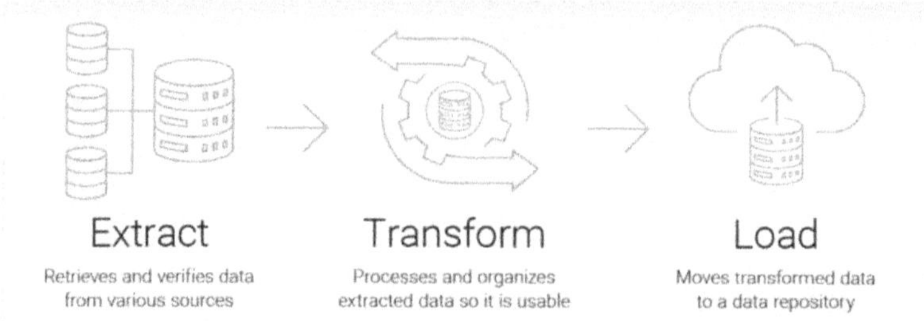

ETL is a three-step process, and each step plays a crucial role in the movement and processing of data. Let's break down these steps:

1. **Extract**: In the "Extract" phase, data is gathered from one or more source systems. Sources can include databases, log files, web services, application data, spreadsheets, and more. The primary goal is to collect raw data for further processing.
2. **Transform**: After extraction, data often requires significant transformation to make it suitable for analysis or storage. This transformation phase involves tasks such as cleaning, structuring, enriching, aggregating, and validating the data. The data is modified as needed to ensure it meets the required quality and format.
3. **Load**: Once data is extracted and transformed, it is loaded into a target system, such as a data warehouse, data lake, or database. The target system is optimized for storage and retrieval, making data readily available for reporting, analytics, and business intelligence.

Lifecycle Phases:

- Requirement gathering
- Data profiling
- ETL design
- Development
- Testing
- Deployment
- Monitoring and maintenance

ETL is a fundamental process for data integration, ensuring that data from diverse sources can be combined and analyzed cohesively. This process allows organizations to harness the full potential of their data, facilitating data-driven decision-making, predictive analytics, and insights generation.

Components of ETL

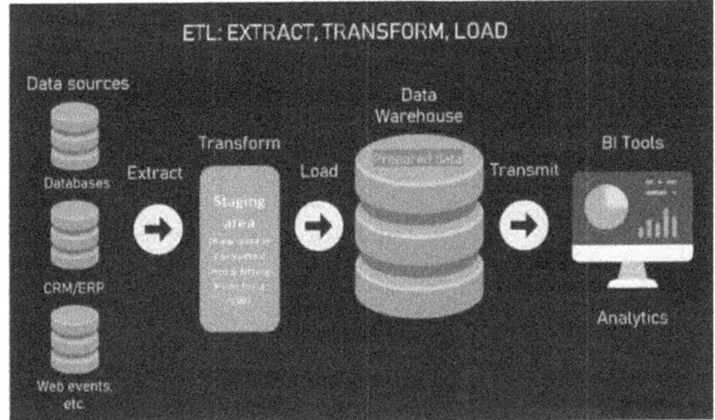

The ETL process involves a series of components, each with specific functions. Let's examine these components in detail:

1. **Data Sources**: Data sources are the origins of the data. They can be internal databases, external databases, flat files, APIs, web services, or log files. Data engineers identify, connect to, and collect data from these sources during the extraction phase.
2. **Data Staging Area**: A staging area serves as an intermediate storage location where data is temporarily held after extraction and before transformation. Staging areas ensure data integrity and provide a buffer for error handling and recovery.
3. **ETL Tools**: ETL tools are software applications or platforms designed for extracting, transforming, and loading data. They provide a range of features, including connectivity to data sources, data transformation functions, and data loading capabilities. Popular ETL tools include Apache Nifi, Talend, Informatica, and Apache Beam.
4. **Data Transformation Logic**: Data transformation involves applying rules and logic to the extracted data to shape it according to the desired format and quality standards. This includes tasks like data cleaning, formatting, aggregation, and calculation.
5. **Target Database or System**: The target system is where transformed data is loaded. This can be a data warehouse, data lake, relational database, or any other storage solution. The target system is optimized for efficient storage and retrieval of data.
6. **ETL Workflow**: ETL workflows are sequences of tasks that define the order and dependencies of ETL

processes. They dictate how data is extracted, transformed, and loaded and ensure that the entire ETL process is orchestrated efficiently.

Challenges in ETL

While ETL is a critical component of data engineering, it comes with its share of challenges:

1. **Data Volume**: Handling large volumes of data can be resource-intensive and may require distributed processing frameworks like Apache Spark or Hadoop.
2. **Data Variety**: Data comes in various formats, including structured, semi-structured, and unstructured. ETL processes must handle this diversity efficiently.
3. **Data Quality**: Ensuring data quality during transformation and loading is a constant challenge. Handling missing, inconsistent, or erroneous data requires robust validation and cleansing procedures.
4. **Latency**: In real-time or near-real-time ETL scenarios, reducing data processing latency is crucial for making timely decisions. Minimizing the time between data extraction and availability is a challenge.
5. **Complex Transformations**: Complex data transformations and business logic may require extensive coding and testing, which can be time-consuming.
6. **Error Handling and Recovery**: ETL processes must be resilient to errors. Handling and recovering from errors, including data validation failures and system failures, is a significant challenge.

7. **Data Security**: Ensuring data security and privacy throughout the ETL process is paramount, particularly when handling sensitive or regulated data.
8. **Scalability**: As data volumes grow, ETL processes must scale to handle the increased load. Scalability is a continuous challenge, particularly in dynamic environments.

Best Practices for ETL

To address the challenges of ETL effectively, data engineers should follow best practices to create robust and efficient data pipelines. Here are some key best practices for ETL:

1. **Data Profiling**: Before beginning the ETL process, conduct data profiling to understand the source data's characteristics, quality, and anomalies. This knowledge informs the transformation and cleansing steps.
2. **Automated Testing**: Implement automated testing for ETL processes to detect and resolve errors early in the pipeline. This includes data validation, data consistency checks, and performance testing.
3. **Modularity**: Design ETL processes with modularity in mind. Break down the process into manageable, reusable components, making it easier to maintain and adapt.
4. **Error Handling and Logging**: Implement comprehensive error handling and logging mechanisms to capture issues and failures. This facilitates troubleshooting and recovery.

5. **Incremental Loading**: When possible, use incremental loading to process only the data that has changed since the last ETL run. This reduces processing time and resource utilization.
6. **Parallel Processing**: Take advantage of parallel processing to distribute the ETL workload across multiple resources, improving performance and scalability.
7. **Metadata Management**: Maintain detailed metadata about the ETL processes, including data lineage, transformation rules, and data dependencies. This metadata aids in tracking data changes and auditing.
8. **Version Control**: Use version control systems to manage ETL code and configurations. This ensures that changes are tracked, and historical versions can be restored if needed.
9. **Data Encryption and Security**: Implement data encryption and security measures to protect data both in transit and at rest. Ensure compliance with data privacy regulations.

10. **Monitoring and Alerts**:

    Set up monitoring and alerting systems to continuously track the health and performance of ETL processes. Proactively address issues as they arise.

ETL in Real-World Scenarios

To illustrate the importance and complexity of ETL, let's consider a real-world scenario: a retail company's ETL process for analyzing sales data.

Data Extraction: The company extracts sales data from various sources, including point-of-sale systems, e-commerce platforms, and customer feedback forms. This data is collected at different intervals, such as daily, hourly, or in near-real-time.

Data Transformation: The extracted data is transformed to ensure consistency and quality. This includes cleaning data to remove duplicates, validating order details, and aggregating sales data by product category.

Data Loading: The cleaned and transformed data is loaded into a data warehouse. The data warehouse is optimized for analytical queries, allowing business analysts to run reports on sales trends, inventory levels, and customer behavior.

Challenges: In this scenario, challenges might include handling data from diverse sources, dealing with inconsistencies in order details, and optimizing data warehouse performance for complex queries.

This example highlights the importance of ETL in a real-world context. ETL processes enable organizations to turn raw, scattered data into actionable insights, supporting data-driven decision-making and business growth.

3.2 ETL Tools and Technologies

Popular ETL tools include:

- **Azure Data Factory (ADF)** – Cloud-based ETL service for orchestrating data workflows

- **Apache NiFi** – Real-time data ingestion and transformation
- **Talend** – Open-source ETL with a visual interface
- **Informatica PowerCenter** – Enterprise-grade ETL platform
- **Databricks** – Unified analytics platform with strong support for big data and machine learning
- **Apache Airflow** – Workflow orchestration tool often used for ETL pipelines

3.3 Building Effective ETL Pipelines

Key principles:

- **Modularity**: Break down pipelines into reusable components
- **Scalability**: Design for large volumes of data
- **Error Handling**: Implement logging, retries, and alerts
- **Performance Optimization**: Use parallel processing, indexing, and caching
- **Data Quality**: Validate and cleanse data at every stage
- **Security**: Encrypt sensitive data and manage access controls

3.4 Hands-On: Building a Complete ETL Pipeline Using ADF and Databricks

Scenario: Load sales data from an on-prem SQL Server to Azure Data Lake, transform it using Databricks, and load it into Azure Synapse Analytics.

Steps:

1. **Extract with ADF**:
    - Create a linked service to SQL Server
    - Define a dataset and pipeline to extract data
    - Store raw data in Azure Data Lake
2. **Transform with Databricks**:
    - Mount the Data Lake in Databricks
    - Use PySpark to clean and transform data
    - Save the transformed data back to Data Lake or directly to Synapse
3. **Load with ADF**:
    - Create a new pipeline to move transformed data to Synapse
    - Schedule and monitor the pipeline

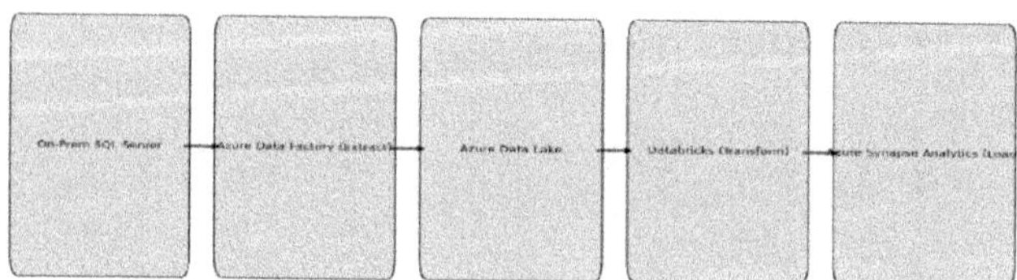

Here's a **step-by-step architecture diagram** for an ETL pipeline using **Azure Data Factory (ADF)** and **Databricks**:

Flow Description:

1. **On-Prem SQL Server**

   Source system containing raw transactional data.

2. **Azure Data Factory (Extract)**

   - Connects to the on-prem SQL Server using a self-hosted integration runtime.
   - Extracts data and moves it to Azure Data Lake.

3. **Azure Data Lake**

   - Stores raw data in a scalable, cost-effective format (e.g., Parquet, CSV).

4. **Databricks (Transform)**

   - Reads raw data from the Data Lake.
   - Applies transformations using PySpark or SQL.
   - Writes the cleaned and enriched data back to the Data Lake or directly to Synapse.

5. **Azure Synapse Analytics (Load)**

- Final destination for transformed data.
- Supports advanced analytics and reporting.

Conclusion

ETL (Extract, Transform, Load) processes are the backbone of data engineering, playing a pivotal role in collecting, preparing, and delivering data for analysis and decision-making. While ETL presents challenges related to data volume, variety, quality, and latency, following best practices can help data engineers create robust and efficient data pipelines. ETL processes are crucial for organizations looking to harness the full potential of their data and gain a competitive edge through data-driven insights.

In the following chapters, we will explore additional aspects of data engineering, including data warehousing, data integration, data quality, and data pipeline optimization. These topics are essential for building resilient and efficient data systems that empower organizations to make informed decisions and drive innovation.

Chapter 4: Data Warehousing and Dimensional Modeling

4.1 Introduction to Data Warehouses

A **Data Warehouse (DW)** is a centralized repository designed for analytical reporting and decision-making. It consolidates data from multiple sources, enabling historical analysis and business intelligence.

Key Characteristics:

- Subject-oriented
- Integrated
- Time-variant
- Non-volatile

Use Cases:

- Business Intelligence (BI)
- Data Mining
- Reporting and Dashboards

The Role of Data Warehousing

Data warehousing is a critical component of data engineering, providing a centralized repository for storing and managing data from various sources. Its primary purpose is to facilitate business intelligence (BI), reporting, and analytics. Unlike operational databases, which are optimized for transactional processing, data warehouses are designed to support complex queries and data analysis.

Key roles of data warehousing include:

1. **Data Integration**: Data warehouses consolidate data from multiple sources, including ETL processes, into a single, unified structure. This integration simplifies data access and analysis.
2. **Data Historical Storage**: Data warehouses often retain historical data, allowing organizations to track trends and changes over time. Historical data is invaluable for understanding long-term business performance.
3. **Performance Optimization**: Data warehouses are optimized for query performance, enabling complex queries and aggregations to be executed efficiently. This performance enhancement is achieved through various techniques, including indexing, compression, and partitioning.

4. **Data Quality Assurance**: Data in a data warehouse is typically cleaned, validated, and transformed during the ETL process. This ensures data quality and consistency.
5. **Data Security**: Data warehouses implement security measures to protect sensitive and confidential data, ensuring that only authorized users can access specific information.

4.2 Data Warehousing Architecture and Solutions

There are different architectural approaches to data warehousing, each of its own, advantages and use cases. Two common data warehousing architectures are:

1. **Enterprise Data Warehouse (EDW)**: The EDW is a centralized repository that stores data from various sources across an entire organization. It is designed to support the diverse data needs of an enterprise. The data in an EDW is typically integrated and transformed during the ETL process to ensure consistency.

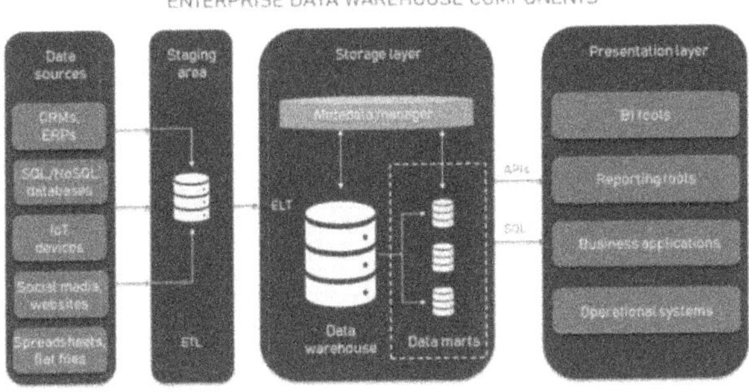

2. **Data Marts**: Data marts are subsets of the EDW designed to serve specific departments, business units,

or use cases within an organization. They are often tailored to meet the unique requirements of a particular group. Data marts can be independent or linked to the central EDW.

Dimensional Modeling

Dimensional modeling is a technique used to design data models within a data warehouse. It is specifically optimized for querying and reporting, making it easier for users to access and analyze data. Dimensional modeling structures data into two main types of tables: fact tables and dimension tables.

Fact Tables: Fact tables contain quantitative data, often referred to as measures or metrics. These measures are typically numerical values, such as sales revenue, quantities sold, or profit margins. Fact tables also include foreign keys that link to dimension tables, providing context for the measures.

Dimension Tables: Dimension tables provide descriptive information about the data in the fact tables. They are often used to filter, group, or slice the data in the fact tables. Examples of dimension tables include customer tables, product tables, and timetables. Dimension tables contain attributes like customer names, product categories, and dates.

Dimensional modeling is characterized by the "star schema" and the "snowflake schema." These schema designs are used to organize fact and dimension tables in a logical structure, optimizing query performance and providing a user-friendly approach to data analysis.

1. **Star Schema**: In a star schema, the fact table is at the center, surrounded by dimension tables. Each

dimension table is directly linked to the fact table through a foreign key. This design simplifies queries and allows for fast access to data. It resembles a star when visualized, with the fact table at the center and dimension tables radiating outwards.

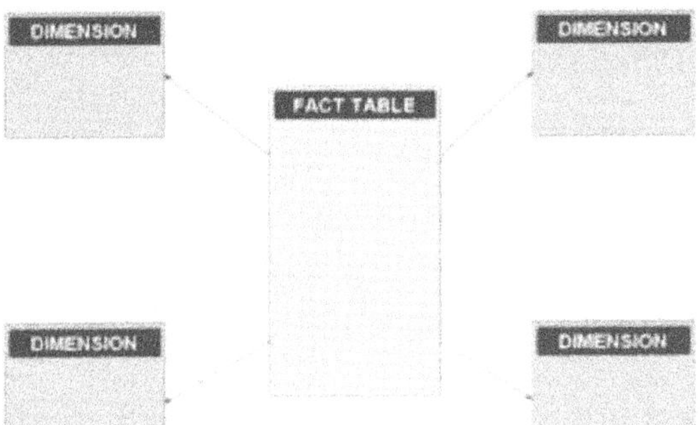

2. **Snowflake Schema**: The snowflake schema is an extension of the star schema. In a snowflake schema, dimension tables are normalized, meaning that they are broken down into additional sub-dimension tables. This design reduces data redundancy but may require more complex queries to retrieve data. It resembles a snowflake when visualized due to the branching structure of dimension tables.

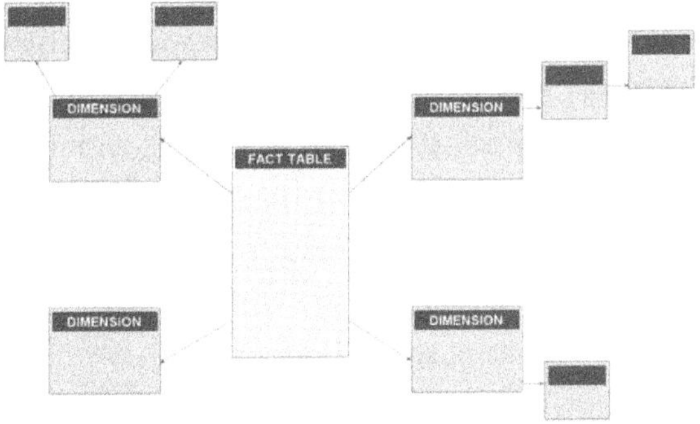

Dimensional modeling enhances the usability of data warehouses, making it easier for business users to navigate and analyze data. It allows for intuitive querying and reporting, enabling users to explore data without needing extensive knowledge of the underlying database structure.

Designing Dimensional Models

Designing effective dimensional models requires careful consideration of the business requirements, the nature of the data, and the expected queries and reports. Here are key steps to designing dimensional models:

1. **Identify Business Processes**: Begin by understanding the business processes that the data warehouse will support. Identify the metrics (measures) and attributes (dimensions) that are relevant to these processes.
2. **Select Dimensions**: Determine which attributes will serve as dimensions in the model. Common dimensions include time, geography, product, customer, and employee. These attributes should help provide context for the measures.
3. **Select Measures**: Choose the measures (quantitative data) that will be stored in the fact table. These measures should align with the identified business processes and objectives.
4. **Define Hierarchies**: Define hierarchies within dimension tables. For example, a time dimension might have hierarchies such as year, quarter, month, and day. These hierarchies help users drill down or roll up data.
5. **Establish Relationships**: Establish relationships between fact tables and dimension tables. Identify which

attributes in the dimension tables serve as foreign keys in the fact table.

6. **Handle Slowly Changing Dimensions (SCDs)**: Address changes in dimension attributes over time, such as customer address updates or product category changes. Implement strategies to manage these changes, including using SCD Type 1 (overwrite), SCD Type 2 (historical), or other techniques.
7. **Validate Model with Users**: Involve end-users and stakeholders in the validation process to ensure that the model aligns with their reporting and analysis needs.

Query Performance and Optimization

Query performance is a critical consideration in data warehousing. Dimensional modeling, when done well, significantly enhances query performance. However, other factors can impact the efficiency of queries, such as the design of the data warehouse, indexing strategies, and database optimization.

Here are some techniques to optimize query performance in data warehousing:

1. **Indexing**: Implement appropriate indexes on fact and dimension tables to speed up query execution. Techniques like bitmap indexing and star transformation can enhance performance.
2. **Partitioning**: Divide large fact tables and dimension tables into smaller partitions, which can be stored and queried more efficiently.

3. **Materialized Views**: Create materialized views to precompute and store the results of commonly used queries. This reduces the time required to generate the results.
4. **Query Tuning**: Regularly monitor and tune queries to identify and address performance bottlenecks. Tools like query optimizers and profiling can help with this process.

Challenges in Data Warehousing and Dimensional Modeling

While data warehousing and dimensional modeling offer significant advantages, they come with their own set of challenges:

1. **Data Integration**: Consolidating data from various sources can be complex and time-consuming. Ensuring data quality and consistency during integration is a continuous challenge.
2. **Data Volume**: Handling large volumes of data in a data warehouse can strain storage and processing resources. Scalability is a critical consideration.
3. **Data Security**: Protecting sensitive data in a data warehouse is essential. Robust security measures, including encryption and access controls, are necessary.
4. **Data Governance**: Establishing data governance practices to ensure data accuracy, compliance, and ethical use is an ongoing challenge.
5. **ETL Complexity**: ETL processes need to be designed and maintained to handle the transformation of data into a dimensional model.

6. **Query Performance**: Ensuring that queries perform efficiently and meet user expectations is a constant consideration.

Typical Architecture Layers:

- **Data Source Layer**: Operational databases, flat files, APIs
- **ETL Layer**: Extract, Transform, Load processes
- **Data Storage Layer**: Star/Snowflake schema models
- **Presentation Layer**: BI tools like Power BI, Tableau

Popular Solutions:

- **Azure Synapse Analytics**
- **Amazon Redshift**
- **Google BigQuery**
- **Snowflake**

Schema Design:

- **Star Schema**: Central fact table linked to dimension tables
- **Snowflake Schema**: Normalized dimensions for complex hierarchies

Real-World Scenario: Retail Analytics

To illustrate the significance of data warehousing and dimensional modeling, let's consider a real-world scenario in retail analytics. A retail company aims to analyze sales data to gain insights into product performance, customer behavior, and inventory management. Here's how data warehousing and dimensional modeling can be applied:

Data Integration: The company collects data from various sources, including point-of-sale systems, e-commerce platforms, and customer surveys. This data is integrated and transformed using ETL processes to ensure consistency and data quality.

Dimensional Modeling: The data warehouse is designed using dimensional modeling principles. Fact tables contain sales metrics, such as revenue and units sold, while dimension tables provide context, including product details, customer demographics, and time hierarchies (e.g., year, quarter, month).

Query and Reporting: Business analysts and data scientists can now query the data warehouse using SQL or business intelligence tools. They can easily analyze sales performance, track customer trends, and generate reports on inventory turnover.

Performance Optimization: To optimize query performance, the data warehouse uses indexing and partitioning. Materialized views are created to accelerate frequently used queries, such as weekly sales reports and customer segmentation analysis.

This retail analytics scenario demonstrates how data warehousing and dimensional modeling enable organizations to make data-driven decisions, improve operational efficiency, and gain a competitive advantage in the market.

4.3 Hands-On: Build a Star-Schema Data Warehouse in Azure Synapse and Load Data Using Python

Scenario:

Create a **Sales Data Warehouse** with the following schema:

- **Fact Table**: fact_sales
- **Dimension Tables**: dim_customer, dim_product, dim_date

Steps:

1. **Define Schema in Synapse**:
    - Create tables using SQL scripts in Synapse Studio.
2. **Prepare Sample Data**:
    - Use CSV files or generate synthetic data for dimensions and facts.
3. **Load Data Using Python**:
    - Use pyodbc or sqlalchemy to connect to Synapse.
    - Load data from local files or Azure Blob Storage.

Chapter 5: Data Integration Strategies and Best Practices

In the previous chapters, we explored the fundamental aspects of data engineering, including data modeling, database design, ETL processes, data warehousing, and dimensional modeling. Now, we turn our attention to data integration, a critical component of data engineering that involves combining data from various sources into a cohesive and unified data store. In this chapter, we will delve into data integration strategies, challenges, and best practices that enable organizations to harness the full potential of their data assets.

The Need for Data Integration

Data integration is the process of combining data from diverse sources into a unified view. In today's data-driven world, organizations deal with a multitude of data sources, including databases, cloud services, external APIs, log files, spreadsheets, and more. These sources may vary in data formats, structures, and storage technologies.

The need for data integration arises from several factors:

1. **Data Silos**: Many organizations have data silos, where different departments or teams manage their data independently. This isolation results in fragmented, redundant, and often inconsistent data.
2. **Data Diversity**: Data can exist in various formats, including structured, semi-structured, and unstructured data. Combining and making sense of such diverse data is a challenge.

3. **Real-Time Data**: Businesses increasingly demand real-time access to data. This requires integration solutions that can handle streaming data from various sources.
4. **Business Insights**: To gain valuable insights, organizations must combine data from different sources to understand customer behavior, market trends, and operational performance comprehensively.
5. **Regulatory Compliance**: Compliance requirements often necessitate the integration of data from multiple systems to provide an accurate and auditable view of data.

5.1 Data Integration Strategies

Data integration involves combining data from different sources to provide a unified view. Common strategies include:

- **ETL (Extract, Transform, Load):** Batch processing for historical data
- **ELT (Extract, Load, Transform):** Used in modern cloud data platforms
- **Data Virtualization:** Real-time access without data movement
- **Change Data Capture (CDC):** Captures and syncs only changed data
- **API-based Integration:** Pulls data from external services in real-time

Data integration can be approached using various strategies, depending on the organization's needs and the characteristics of the data sources. Here are some common data integration strategies:

1. **Batch Processing**: Batch processing involves collecting and processing data in predefined batches or time intervals. It is suitable for scenarios where data latency is not a critical concern, such as nightly ETL jobs or periodic data synchronization.
2. **Real-Time Data Integration**: In real-time data integration, data is ingested and processed as soon as it becomes available. This approach is ideal for applications that require up-to-the-minute insights, such as fraud detection, IoT monitoring, or stock market analysis.
3. **Change Data Capture (CDC)**: CDC is a technique for identifying and capturing changes made to data sources. It tracks inserts, updates, and deletes, ensuring that only changed data is replicated or integrated. CDC is commonly used for near-real-time data integration.
4. **Federated Data Integration**: Federated data integration allows data to remain in its original location, with integration tools providing a unified view. This strategy is useful when migrating all data to a central repository is not feasible or when dealing with sensitive data.
5. **Data Virtualization**: Data virtualization creates a virtual layer that abstracts data sources, enabling users to query and access data without physically moving it. It simplifies data access and provides a unified view without the need for ETL processes.

Challenges in Data Integration

Data integration presents several challenges that organizations must address to ensure the success of their data engineering efforts. Common challenges include:

1. **Data Quality**: Maintaining data quality is a significant challenge, as data from different sources may contain errors, inconsistencies, or missing values. Data cleansing and validation are essential.
2. **Data Transformation**: Transforming data into a common format or schema is often required. Data engineers must implement transformations that preserve data integrity and maintain compatibility.
3. **Data Latency**: Balancing the trade-off between real-time data integration and batch processing is challenging. Real-time integration can introduce latency, while batch processing may not meet real-time requirements.
4. **Data Volume**: Handling large volumes of data efficiently requires scalable infrastructure and optimized data processing techniques. Data volume can strain resources and impact performance.
5. **Data Security and Privacy**: Protecting sensitive data during integration is paramount. Compliance with data privacy regulations, such as GDPR, HIPAA, or CCPA, is a continuous concern.
6. **Data Governance**: Establishing data governance practices ensures data accuracy, accountability, and compliance. Data lineage, audit trails, and data access controls are essential components.
7. **Diverse Data Sources**: Data can come in various formats and structures. Integrating these diverse sources while preserving data fidelity can be complex.

Best Practices for Data Integration

To overcome the challenges of data integration, organizations should follow best practices that ensure the efficiency, accuracy, and security of integrated data. Here are key best practices for data integration:

1. **Data Profiling**: Before integration, perform data profiling to understand the quality and characteristics of data sources. This insight helps identify potential issues and transformations needed.
2. **Data Standardization**: Standardize data formats, naming conventions, and coding practices to ensure consistency across data sources. This simplifies integration and enhances data quality.
3. **ETL Processes**: Implement well-defined ETL processes to extract, transform, and load data. ETL tools and workflows help automate and streamline the integration process.
4. **Data Catalogs**: Maintain a data catalog that documents metadata, data lineage, and data dictionaries. This documentation aids in understanding data sources and their integration requirements.
5. **Data Validation**: Use data validation techniques to identify and correct data anomalies. Implement data quality checks and validation rules during integration.
6. **Data Security**: Implement robust data security measures, including encryption, access controls, and identity management, to protect sensitive data during integration.
7. **Data Governance**: Establish data governance practices to ensure data accuracy, compliance, and ethical use. Data stewards can help oversee data integration processes.

8. **Monitoring and Logging**: Implement monitoring and logging of data integration processes. This enables real-time tracking of data movement and performance.
9. **Version Control**: Apply version control to data integration code, configurations, and workflows to track changes and ensure reproducibility.
10. **Scalability**: Design integration processes to scale with growing data volumes. Use distributed processing frameworks and cloud-based solutions for elasticity.

Data Integration Tools and Platforms

Data integration tools and platforms play a crucial role in simplifying and automating the integration process. Some popular data integration tools and platforms include:

1. **Apache Nifi**: An open-source data integration tool for automating data ingestion and ETL processes.
2. **Talend**: A comprehensive data integration platform that supports ETL, data quality, and data governance.
3. **Informatica**: A data integration and data quality platform that offers a wide range of integration capabilities.
4. **Microsoft SQL Server Integration Services (SSIS)**: A Microsoft tool for ETL processes that integrates with SQL Server.
5. **Apache Kafka**: A distributed streaming platform that is often used for real-time data integration and event-driven architectures.
6. **AWS Glue**: Amazon's ETL service for preparing and loading data for analytics.

Real-World Scenario: Customer 360 Integration

To illustrate the importance of data integration, let's consider a real-world scenario in which a retail company aims to create a 360-degree view of its customers. The goal is to integrate data from various sources to understand customer behavior and preferences comprehensively.

Data Sources: Data sources include customer databases, e-commerce platforms, social media interactions, and customer service logs. Each source contains data in different formats and structures.

Data Integration: The company uses a data integration platform to ingest, transform, and load data from these sources. ETL processes are designed to handle data cleansing, transformation, and data quality checks.

Data Warehouse: The integrated data is stored in a data warehouse, which follows a dimensional modeling approach. Dimension tables represent customer attributes, while fact tables capture customer interactions and transactions.

Data Access: Business analysts and marketing teams can access the data warehouse to run queries and generate reports on customer segmentation, lifetime value, and purchasing patterns. The integrated data provides a comprehensive view of customer behavior.

Challenges: Challenges in this scenario include data quality issues, data latency, and ensuring data privacy compliance. However, the integration process enables the organization to gain valuable insights into customer behavior, driving targeted marketing campaigns and improving customer satisfaction.

5.2 Real-time Data Integration with Streaming

Real-time integration enables immediate processing of data as it arrives.

Key Technologies:

- **Apache Kafka**: Distributed event streaming platform
- **Apache Spark Streaming / Structured Streaming**: Scalable stream processing
- **Azure Event Hubs**: Ingests millions of events per second
- **Azure Synapse**: Supports real-time analytics with dedicated SQL pools

Use Cases:

- IoT telemetry
- Financial transactions
- Social media feeds
- Real-time dashboards

3. Hands-On: Stream Data from External APIs into Azure Synapse Using Databricks Spark Streaming

Scenario:

Stream live data (e.g., cryptocurrency prices, weather, or stock market data) from a public API into Azure Synapse using Databricks.

Architecture:

1. **Databricks Notebook**:
    - Uses requests or http.client to poll an API
    - Converts data into a Spark DataFrame
    - Writes to Azure Synapse using JDBC
2. **Azure Synapse**:
    - Stores the streamed data in a dedicated SQL pool
    - Enables real-time analytics and visualization

Conclusion

Data integration is a fundamental component of data engineering, enabling organizations to consolidate and unify data from diverse sources into a cohesive and accessible data store. In an era of data-driven decision-making, efficient data integration is crucial for gaining valuable insights and maintaining a competitive edge.

To address the challenges of data integration, organizations should adopt best practices, implement data integration tools and platforms, and prioritize data quality, security, and governance. With effective data integration, organizations can create a unified view of their data, supporting informed decision-making and innovation.

Chapter 6: Data Quality and Data Governance

6.1 Ensuring Data Quality

Data quality refers to the condition of your data based on various dimensions that define how accurate, consistent, and reliable it is. Ensuring high-quality data is essential for making informed business decisions, as poor-quality data can lead to faulty analytics, unreliable insights, and business risks.

OR

Data quality refers to the condition of data based on factors such as accuracy, completeness, reliability, and relevance.

Key Dimensions:

- **Accuracy**: Data reflects real-world values
- **Completeness**: No missing or null values
- **Consistency**: Uniform format and values across datasets
- **Timeliness**: Data is up-to-date
- **Validity**: Data conforms to defined formats and rules

Techniques:

- Data profiling
- Validation rules

- Anomaly detection
- Automated quality checks

6.1.1 Dimensions of Data Quality

1. **Accuracy:** Data should correctly represent the real-world object or event it describes.
    - Example: A customer's name in the database should match their legal name.
2. **Completeness:** All required data fields should be populated.
    - Example: If an email address is a mandatory field, there should be no missing entries in that column.
3. **Consistency:** Data should be consistent across systems and datasets.
    - Example: If a customer's address is stored in two systems, the data should be identical in both.
4. **Validity:** Data should conform to predefined formats and rules.
    - Example: A date field should follow the correct date format (YYYY-MM-DD).

5. **Timeliness:** Data should be up to date and available when needed.
    - Example: Sales data should be processed and available for analysis shortly after transactions are completed.
6. **Uniqueness:** There should be no duplicate records.
    - Example: Each customer should be represented only once in the database.

6.1.2 Data Quality Issues and Impacts

Common Data Quality Issues:

- Missing values
- Inconsistent formats (e.g., different date formats)
- Duplicated records
- Out-of-date information

Impacts of Poor Data Quality:

- Misleading business insights
- Inefficient processes and wasted resources
- Loss of trust in data-driven decision-making
- Non-compliance with regulations

6.1.3 Practical Example: Implementing Data Quality Checks

Let's implement some basic data quality checks using Python and Pandas.

Example Code: Data Quality Checks in Python

```
import pandas as pd

# Sample dataset
data = {
    'CustomerID': [101, 102, 103, 104, None],
    'CustomerName': ['John Doe', 'Jane Smith', None, 'Alice Brown', 'Chris Green'],
    'Email': ['john@example.com', None, 'jane@example.com', 'alice@example.com', 'chris@example.com'],
    'DateOfBirth': ['1985-05-10', '1990-07-22', 'INVALID_DATE', '1975-09-15', '1988-12-01']
}

df = pd.DataFrame(data)

# 1. Check for missing values
missing_values = df.isnull().sum()
print("Missing values:\n", missing_values)

# 2. Check for invalid date formats
def is_valid_date(date):
    try:
        pd.to_datetime(date)
        return True
    except ValueError:
        return False

df['ValidDateOfBirth'] = df['DateOfBirth'].apply(is_valid_date)
invalid_dates = df[df['ValidDateOfBirth'] == False]
print("Invalid dates:\n", invalid_dates)
```

Continue for 3rd step for duplicate see the next screen shot for all 3 step in single screen.

In this example, we check for missing values, validate date formats, and detect duplicate records. This is a basic illustration of data quality checks that can be extended to more complex scenarios.

```python
# 1. Check for missing values
missing_values = df.isnull().sum()
print("Missing values:\n", missing_values)

# 2. Check for invalid date formats
def is_valid_date(date):
    try:
        pd.to_datetime(date)
        return True
    except ValueError:
        return False

df['ValidDateOfBirth'] = df['DateOfBirth'].apply(is_valid_date)
invalid_dates = df[df['ValidDateOfBirth'] == False]
print("Invalid dates:\n", invalid_dates)

# 3. Check for duplicate records
duplicates = df[df.duplicated()]
print("Duplicate records:\n", duplicates)
```

6.2 Data Governance Principles & Best Practices

Data governance is the process of managing the availability, usability, integrity, and security of the data used in an organization. It establishes clear policies for handling data and ensures that the data is consistent, trustworthy, and compliant with relevant regulations.

Data governance ensures that data is managed properly across its lifecycle.

Core Principles:

- **Accountability**: Clear ownership and stewardship
- **Transparency**: Documented policies and procedures

- **Compliance**: Adherence to regulations (e.g., GDPR, HIPAA)
- **Security**: Controlled access and encryption
- **Standardization**: Consistent definitions and formats

Best Practices:

- Establish a data governance council
- Define data policies and standards
- Use metadata management tools
- Monitor and audit data usage

6.2.1 Key Components of Data Governance

1. **Data Stewardship:** Assigning roles and responsibilities for managing data across its lifecycle.
    - Example: A data steward ensures that the customer data in the CRM system is up to date and accurate.
2. **Data Policies and Standards:** Defining rules and guidelines for data access, usage, and quality.
    - Example: Policies for who can access sensitive data and how data should be secured.

3. **Data Lineage:** Tracking the journey of data from its source to its final destination.
    - Example: Knowing how sales data moves from a transactional database into a data warehouse and finally into a BI dashboard.
4. **Data Cataloging:** Creating an organized inventory of data assets across the organization.
    - Example: Using a data catalog to track datasets, their locations, and their owners.
5. **Data Compliance and Security:** Ensuring data practices meet regulatory requirements (e.g., GDPR, HIPAA) and are secured against breaches.
    - Example: Encrypting personally identifiable information (PII) and controlling who can access it.

6.2.2 Importance of Data Governance

- **Trustworthy Data:** By defining processes and roles, data governance ensures data is consistent and trustworthy.
- **Regulatory Compliance:** Data governance helps organizations comply with laws and regulations (e.g., GDPR, HIPAA).

- **Data Security:** By enforcing access controls and security protocols, it protects data from unauthorized access or breaches.
- **Improved Data Management:** Governance frameworks standardize the way data is handled across the organization.

6.2.3 Practical Example: Using Azure Purview for Data Governance

Azure Purview is a unified data governance solution that helps organizations manage and catalog data across on-premises, multi-cloud, and SaaS environments.

Steps to Implement Data Governance with Azure Purview:

1. **Set Up Azure Purview**
    - Go to the Azure Portal.
    - Search for **Azure Purview** and create a Purview account.
    - Once the account is created, navigate to the **Azure Purview Studio**.
2. **Data Cataloging**
    - In Purview Studio, you can scan data sources (e.g., Azure Data Lake, Synapse, SQL databases) to automatically catalog data.

- After the scan, you will see all the datasets and assets organized by data type, source, and usage.

3. **Data Lineage Tracking**

   - Azure Purview automatically tracks the movement of data across different services.

   - You can visualize how data flows from one system (e.g., Data Lake) into another (e.g., Synapse) and analyze transformations that occur along the way.

4. **Data Governance Policies**

   - Create and manage governance policies that define who can access specific data, how it should be used, and under what conditions.

   - Example: Restricting access to customer PII data to only authorized personnel.

Purview Example Diagram: Data Lineage

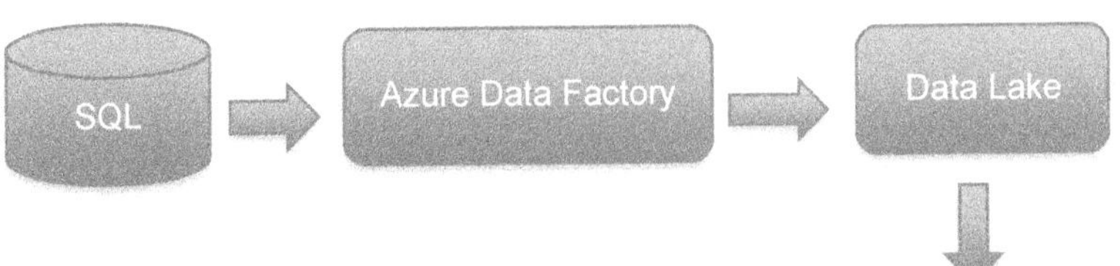

Power BI

The diagram above shows the lineage of customer data flowing from a SQL database through Azure Data Factory, into Data Lake Storage, and finally being visualized in Power BI.

6.3 Data Lineage and Data Catalogs

Data Lineage helps you trace the origins of data, its movement, and transformations across systems. It is essential for debugging, auditing, and ensuring the correctness of data pipelines.

Data Catalogs organize and classify datasets, making it easier for users to discover and understand data assets.

6.3.1 Practical Example: Tracking Data Lineage with Databricks

In this example, we will track data lineage using **Databricks** and **Azure Purview**.

Step 1: Integrate Databricks with Azure Purview

1. Set up Databricks on Azure.

2. Use the **Purview Spark connector** to send lineage information from Databricks transformations into Azure Purview.

```
# Databricks notebook
from pyspark.sql import SparkSession

# Initialize Spark session
spark = SparkSession.builder.appName("DataLineageExample").getOrCreate()

# Read data from Azure Data Lake
df = spark.read.csv("abfss://<container>@<storage-account>.dfs.core.windows.net/sales_data.csv", header=True)

# Perform transformation
df_filtered = df.filter(df['region'] == 'North America')

# Save transformed data back to Data Lake
df_filtered.write.csv("abfss://<container>@<storage-account>.dfs.core.windows.net/sales_data_filtered.csv")

# Send lineage information to Azure Purview
# (Assume Azure Purview connector is already configured in the environment)
```

3. View the data lineage in Azure Purview, where you can trace how the sales data moved from Data Lake, was transformed in Databricks, and stored back in the lake.

6.4 Ensuring Data Compliance

Compliance ensures that data handling meets legal and regulatory requirements. In Azure, you can enforce compliance by setting policies for data security, privacy, and access control.

6.4.1 Encryption and Access Control

- **Encryption at Rest:** Use Azure Data Lake's encryption features to secure data at rest.
- **Access Control:** Implement Role-Based Access Control (RBAC) to limit access to sensitive data.

Example: Configuring Encryption and Access Control in Azure

1. **Enable Encryption:**
   - In the Azure Portal, go to your **Storage Account** > **Settings** > **Encryption**.
   - Enable server-side encryption using a customer-managed key (CMK) stored in Azure Key Vault.
2. **Set Up RBAC:**
   - In the Azure Portal, navigate to the **Access Control (IAM)** section of your storage account.
   - Add users and assign them roles such as **Storage Blob Data Contributor** or **Storage Blob Data Reader** to control access to data in Data Lake.

Data Quality Best Practices

To ensure data quality, organizations should implement best practices that span the entire data lifecycle. These practices address data collection, storage, transformation, and analysis. Here are key data quality best practices:

1. **Data Profiling**: Perform data profiling to assess the quality, completeness, and structure of data sources. Identify data quality issues early in the process.
2. **Data Cleaning**: Implement data cleaning procedures to correct errors, remove duplicates, and fill missing data.

Cleaning is a crucial step in the data transformation process.

3. **Data Validation**: Define validation rules to ensure that data conforms to predefined standards. Data validation checks can identify anomalies and errors.
4. **Data Standardization**: Standardize data formats, units, and naming conventions to improve consistency and simplify data integration.
5. **Data Quality Metrics**: Define data quality metrics and key performance indicators (KPIs) to measure and monitor data quality continuously.
6. **Data Quality Tools**: Utilize data quality tools and software to automate data profiling, cleansing, and validation.
7. **Metadata Management**: Document and maintain metadata that describes the source, structure, and lineage of data. Metadata aids in understanding data assets.
8. **Data Ownership**: Assign data ownership and responsibility to data stewards who oversee data quality and compliance.
9. **Data Governance Framework**: Implement a data governance framework that includes policies, procedures, and roles to ensure that data quality and compliance are managed effectively.

Data Governance Best Practices

Effective data governance is integral to ensuring data quality, security, and compliance. Here are best practices for implementing data governance:

1. **Establish Data Governance Council**: Create a data governance council or committee responsible for defining data governance policies and overseeing their implementation.
2. **Define Data Governance Policies**: Develop clear and comprehensive data governance policies that cover data quality, privacy, security, and compliance with relevant regulations.
3. **Data Classification**: Classify data based on its sensitivity, impact on the organization, and regulatory requirements. This classification guides data protection measures.
4. **Data Auditing and Monitoring**: Implement data auditing and monitoring solutions to track data access, changes, and usage. Regular audits help identify and rectify data quality and compliance issues.
5. **Data Privacy Compliance**: Ensure compliance with data protection regulations, such as GDPR, HIPAA, or CCPA. Implement data privacy measures like consent management and data anonymization.
6. **Data Access Controls**: Enforce access controls and permissions to safeguard data. Role-based access and encryption are examples of security measures that restrict unauthorized data access.
7. **Data Documentation**: Maintain comprehensive data documentation that includes metadata, data lineage, and data dictionaries. This documentation aids in data discovery and understanding.
8. **Data Governance Tools**: Utilize data governance tools and platforms that assist in data cataloging, metadata management, and policy enforcement.

4. Hands-On: Implement Data Quality Checks with Python and Monitor Data Lineage Using Azure Purview

Part A: Data Quality Checks with Python

Use Python to:

- Load a dataset (e.g., CSV)
- Check for missing values, duplicates, and outliers
- Validate data types and formats
- Generate a quality report

Part B: Monitor Data Lineage with Azure Purview

Steps:

1. Register your data sources in Azure Purview
2. Scan the sources to extract metadata
3. Visualize data lineage through the Purview Studio
4. Tag and classify sensitive data

Chapter 7: Data Pipeline Optimization

In this chapter, we will focus on optimizing an existing ETL pipeline using **Databricks** and **Azure Data Factory (ADF)**. We'll explore performance tuning techniques, optimize resource utilization, and set up monitoring tools to track pipeline performance. The goal is to make your ETL process faster, more efficient, and easier to maintain.

---

7. 1. Optimizing Data Processing Pipelines

Optimization ensures that data pipelines are efficient, cost-effective, and scalable.

Key Techniques:

- **Partitioning**: Split data for parallel processing
- **Caching**: Store intermediate results to avoid re-computation
- **Predicate Pushdown**: Filter data early in the pipeline
- **Efficient File Formats**: Use Parquet or Delta over CSV
- **Minimize Shuffles**: Avoid wide transformations in Spark

7.1 Key Principles of Data Pipeline Optimization

Before diving into the practical example, let's review some of the key principles for optimizing an ETL pipeline:

1. **Parallelism:** Maximize throughput by processing data in parallel across different stages of the pipeline.
2. **Partitioning:** Break down large datasets into smaller, manageable partitions to improve query and processing performance.
3. **Caching:** Cache intermediate results in memory (e.g., in Spark) to avoid redundant data processing.
4. **Efficient Data Formats:** Use optimized data storage formats such as **Parquet** or **ORC** to reduce storage space and improve read/write performance.
5. **Resource Allocation:** Allocate appropriate resources (compute, memory) to avoid over- or under-provisioning of resources.
6. **Monitoring and Logging:** Implement tools to monitor the pipeline's performance and log issues to track and resolve bottlenecks efficiently.

7.2 Practical Example: Optimize an Existing ETL Pipeline Using Databricks and ADF

In this practical example, we will optimize an ETL pipeline that reads data from Azure Data Lake, processes it in Databricks using Apache Spark, and loads it into an Azure Synapse Analytics data warehouse. We will also set up monitoring tools in ADF to track performance metrics.

Scenario Overview

- **Source Data:** Raw sales transaction data stored in **Azure Data Lake** (in CSV format).
- **Transformation:** Perform data cleansing and aggregation in **Databricks** using Spark.
- **Destination:** Store the cleaned and aggregated data in **Azure Synapse Analytics**.
- **Optimization Goal:** Improve the speed and efficiency of the pipeline while maintaining data quality.

7.2.1 Step 1: Existing ETL Pipeline Overview

The existing ETL pipeline is implemented in **Azure Data Factory** and **Databricks**:

1. **Data Ingestion:** ADF pipeline ingests raw sales data from Azure Data Lake.
2. **Transformation:** The data is processed in Databricks using a **Notebook** that performs data cleaning and transformation.
3. **Data Load:** The transformed data is loaded into an **Azure Synapse Analytics** data warehouse.

Pipeline Diagram:

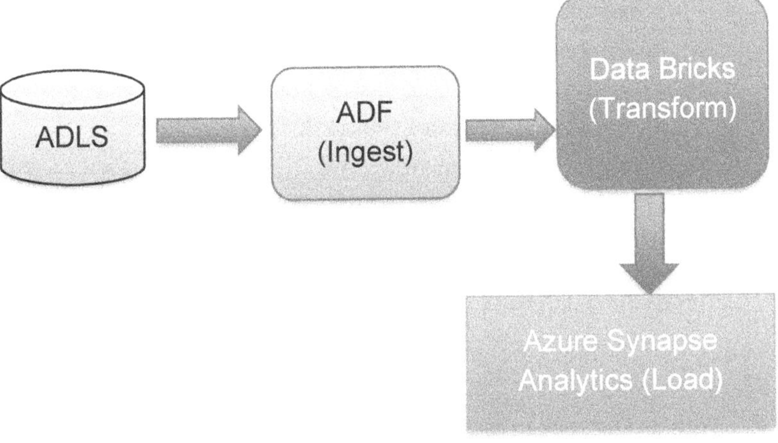

7.2.2 Step 2: Identify Bottlenecks

The first step in optimization is to identify potential bottlenecks. Common areas to investigate include:

- **Data I/O:** Reading and writing large datasets from Azure Data Lake can be slow.
- **Spark Transformations:** Inefficient transformations can cause high memory and CPU usage.

- **Resource Allocation:** Over-provisioned or under-provisioned Databricks clusters can lead to inefficiency.

Monitoring Spark Jobs:

In Databricks, you can use the Spark UI to identify slow-running tasks, stages, and jobs. Pay attention to:

- **Job Execution Time:** Identify stages that take a long time to complete.
- **Task Parallelism:** Ensure that tasks are evenly distributed across available cores.
- **Shuffle Operations:** Minimize shuffle operations as they are expensive in terms of time and resources.

7.2.3 Step 3: Optimize the Databricks Pipeline

We will optimize the data transformation step in Databricks by:

1. **Partitioning the Data:** Partitioning helps distribute the load across multiple workers and reduces data shuffling during processing.
2. **Using the Parquet Format:** Parquet is a columnar storage format that is more efficient than CSV, leading to faster read/write operations.
3. **Caching Intermediate Results:** We'll use caching to avoid reprocessing the same data multiple times within the same pipeline.

Optimized Databricks Code Example:

```python
from pyspark.sql import SparkSession
from pyspark.sql.functions import col

# Initialize Spark session
spark = SparkSession.builder.appName("OptimizedETL").getOrCreate()

# Read data from Azure Data Lake (assumed as CSV format)
raw_data_path = "abfss://<container>@<storage-account>.dfs.core.windows.net/sales_data.csv"
sales_df = spark.read.csv(raw_data_path, header=True, inferSchema=True)

# Optimize: Write data in Parquet format to reduce future I/O time
optimized_data_path = "abfss://<container>@<storage-account>.dfs.core.windows.net/sales_data_optimized.parquet"
sales_df.write.mode("overwrite").parquet(optimized_data_path)

# Read optimized data in Parquet format
sales_df = spark.read.parquet(optimized_data_path)

# Optimize: Partition data by a frequently queried column (e.g., Region)
sales_df = sales_df.repartition("Region")

# Transformation: Perform data cleaning and aggregation
# Example: Filter out invalid data and calculate total sales per region
cleaned_df = sales_df.filter(col("Quantity") > 0).groupBy("Region").agg({"SalesAmount": "sum"})

# Optimize: Cache the intermediate results to avoid reprocessing
cleaned_df.cache()
```

```python
# Load data into Azure Synapse Analytics
synapse_jdbc_url = "jdbc:sqlserver://<synapse-server-name>.database.windows.net:1433;database=<synapse-database>"
cleaned_df.write \
    .format("com.databricks.spark.sqldw") \
    .option("url", synapse_jdbc_url) \
    .option("dbtable", "SalesSummary") \
    .option("user", "<your-username>") \
    .option("password", "<your-password>") \
    .mode("overwrite") \
    .save()
```

Key Optimizations:

1. **Parquet Format:** Reduces the time spent reading and writing data.

2. **Partitioning:** Helps distribute data processing across multiple workers.

3. **Caching:** Saves intermediate results to avoid redundant computation.

7.2.4 Step 4: Optimize Resource Allocation in Databricks

Right-sizing Clusters:

- Use **autoscaling** to dynamically adjust the cluster size based on workload.
- Adjust the **number of worker nodes** and the type of **virtual machines (VMs)** to match the size of your dataset and the complexity of the transformations.

Cluster Configuration Example:

```
Cluster Configuration:
  - Worker Nodes: 4-8 (autoscaling enabled)
  - VM Type: Standard_DS3_v2
  - Databricks Runtime: 10.4 LTS (includes Apache Spark 3.x)
```

Monitor cluster utilization to ensure you are not under- or over-provisioning resources.

7.2.5 Step 5: Set Up Monitoring in Azure Data Factory

Azure Data Factory provides built-in tools to monitor and track the performance of your ETL pipelines. This step involves setting up alerts and monitoring for key performance metrics, such as data load time and resource consumption.

Steps to Set Up Monitoring:

1. **Enable Pipeline Monitoring in ADF:**
    - In the ADF **Monitor** tab, you can track the status of pipeline runs, activity execution, and data movement.
    - You can filter pipeline runs by status (Succeeded, Failed, In Progress) and view detailed logs.
2. **Set Up Alerts and Notifications:**
    - Go to the **Monitor** tab in Azure Data Factory.
    - Set up alerts for specific pipeline failures or execution delays. For example, send an email if a pipeline run takes more than 1 hour.

Example of an Alert Condition:

- **Condition:** Pipeline execution time exceeds 60 minutes.
- **Action:** Send an email notification to the administrator.

3. **Monitor Data Flow Performance:**
    - ADF provides a detailed breakdown of data flow performance. You can view metrics such as data read/write speed, transformation time, and CPU/memory usage.

Monitoring Diagram:

```
+--------------------------------------------------------+
|     Azure Data Factory Pipeline Monitoring             |
|     +--------------------------------------------+     |
|     |  Data Source  --> Ingest --> Transform     |     |
|     |             --> Load --> Monitor           |     |
|     +--------------------------------------------+     |
|                                                        |
|     Alerts:                                            |
|     - Execution Time Exceeds 60 minutes                |
|     - Data Load Errors                                 |
+--------------------------------------------------------+
```

7.2.6 Step 6: Analyze and Improve Pipeline Performance

Once monitoring is in place, use the performance data to further optimize the pipeline. Key metrics to track include:

1. **Data Processing Time:** Analyze how long each stage of the ETL process takes and identify potential slowdowns.
2. **Cluster Utilization:** Monitor resource utilization (CPU, memory) to ensure efficient use of Databricks clusters.
3. **Success/Failure Rates:** Track how often the pipeline succeeds or fails and investigate common points of failure.

7.3 Summary and Best Practices

In this practical example, we optimized an existing ETL pipeline using Databricks and Azure Data Factory by:

- **Using Optimized File Formats:** Switching from CSV to Parquet significantly reduced the time required for data I/O operations.
- **Partitioning and Caching:** Partitioning data and caching intermediate results in Databricks helped distribute workload and avoid redundant computation.
- **Resource Allocation:** Dynamically autoscaling Databricks clusters ensured efficient resource usage.
- **Monitoring and Alerts:** Setting up ADF monitoring allowed us to track pipeline performance and set up alerts to quickly identify issues.

By following these optimization techniques, you can improve the performance, scalability, and reliability of your ETL pipelines.

The Role of Data Pipelines

Data pipelines play a pivotal role in data engineering, providing a structured and automated way to collect, transport, and process data. They enable organizations to:

1. **Ingest Data**: Data pipelines collect data from diverse sources, including databases, web services, log files, and IoT devices.

2. **Transform Data**: Data can be cleansed, enriched, and transformed within pipelines to ensure it is in the desired format and quality.
3. **Store Data**: Pipelines load data into storage systems such as data warehouses, data lakes, or other databases, making it accessible for analysis.
4. **Process Data**: Data pipelines can perform real-time or batch processing on data, making it suitable for various analytical and operational use cases.
5. **Ensure Data Quality**: Data quality checks can be incorporated into data pipelines to identify and address data issues as part of the data flow.
6. **Automate Workflows**: Data pipelines automate the flow of data, reducing manual effort and ensuring consistency in data processing.

Challenges in Data Pipeline Optimization

While data pipelines are a fundamental component of data engineering, they come with their own set of challenges. Addressing these challenges is crucial to ensure that data pipelines are efficient and reliable:

1. **Data Volume**: Handling large volumes of data efficiently can strain the infrastructure and impact performance. Scalability is a critical consideration.
2. **Data Latency**: Balancing real-time data processing with batch processing is a challenge. Latency in data pipelines can hinder timely decision-making.
3. **Data Complexity**: Dealing with data in different formats, structures, and sources requires flexibility and robust data integration techniques.

4. **Data Transformation**: The complexity of data transformations can slow down pipelines. Optimizing these transformations is essential for efficiency.
5. **Error Handling**: Data pipelines need mechanisms for error handling, data recovery, and notifications to ensure data reliability.
6. **Data Monitoring**: Monitoring the health and performance of data pipelines in real-time is essential. Identifying and addressing issues as they occur is critical.

Strategies for Data Pipeline Optimization

To overcome the challenges of data pipeline optimization, organizations can employ various strategies and best practices. Here are key strategies to optimize data pipelines:

1. **Data Partitioning**: Partitioning data into smaller, manageable units based on specific attributes, such as date or category, enables parallel processing and accelerates data retrieval.
2. **Distributed Processing**: Utilize distributed computing frameworks, such as Apache Hadoop or Apache Spark, to process data in parallel across a cluster of machines.
3. **Data Compression**: Compress data before transmission and storage to reduce storage costs and improve data transfer times.
4. **Caching**: Implement caching mechanisms to store frequently accessed data, reducing the need to retrieve it from the source each time.
5. **Data Pipeline Orchestration**: Use data pipeline orchestration tools like Apache Airflow or Luigi to

schedule and manage pipeline workflows, ensuring dependencies are met and processes run efficiently.

6. **Data Pipeline Monitoring**: Implement real-time monitoring and alerting systems to track the health and performance of data pipelines. This allows for proactive issue resolution.
7. **Data Quality Checks**: Embed data quality checks and validation steps within the pipeline to identify and address data anomalies and issues as part of the data flow.
8. **Dynamic Scaling**: Leverage cloud computing and serverless technologies to dynamically scale resources based on data processing demand, optimizing cost and performance.
9. **Data Lineage and Documentation**: Maintain data lineage and comprehensive documentation to track the flow and transformations of data, aiding in debugging and understanding the pipeline.
10. **Optimize Data Storage**: Choose appropriate data storage solutions, including databases, data lakes, and cloud storage, based on the specific needs of the pipeline.

Data Pipeline Tools and Frameworks

Data pipeline optimization often involves the use of specialized tools and frameworks that streamline data movement and processing. Here are some popular data pipeline tools and frameworks:

1. **Apache NiFi**: An open-source data integration tool for designing data flows and automating data ingestion and transformation.

2. **Apache Kafka**: A distributed streaming platform that is often used for real-time data integration and event-driven architectures.
3. **Apache Airflow**: An open-source platform to programmatically author, schedule, and monitor data pipelines.
4. **Luigi**: A Python-based framework for building complex data pipelines and workflows.
5. **Talend**: A data integration and ETL tool that provides a wide range of data pipeline capabilities.
6. **AWS Glue**: Amazon's ETL service for preparing and loading data for analytics in the cloud.
7. **Google Cloud Dataflow**: A fully managed service for processing real-time and batch data.
8. **Microsoft Azure Data Factory**: A cloud-based data integration service that allows you to create data-driven workflows.

Hands-On Assignment:

1. Implement a simple ETL pipeline using ADF and Databricks.

2. Optimize the pipeline by partitioning data, using the Parquet format, and caching results.

3. Set up monitoring in Azure Data Factory and configure alerts to notify you of any performance issues.

Hands-On Assignment: Implement and Optimize an ETL Pipeline using Azure Data Factory (ADF) and Databricks

This hands-on assignment will guide you through implementing a simple ETL pipeline using **Azure Data Factory (ADF)** and **Databricks**, optimizing it with best practices such as partitioning, using the **Parquet** format, and caching results. Finally, you'll learn how to set up monitoring in ADF and configure alerts to track pipeline performance and notify you of any issues.

Objectives:

By completing this assignment, you will:

1. Build a simple ETL pipeline that ingests raw data from **Azure Data Lake**, transforms it using **Databricks**, and loads it into **Azure Synapse Analytics**.

2. Optimize the pipeline by using the **Parquet** format, partitioning data, and caching intermediate results.

3. Set up monitoring in **Azure Data Factory** and configure alerts to notify you of any performance issues.

Prerequisites:

1. An active **Azure account** with access to **Azure Data Factory**, **Databricks**, and **Azure Synapse Analytics**.

2. Basic knowledge of **Apache Spark** and **Python**.

3. Raw data available in **Azure Data Lake Storage (ADLS)** in **CSV format**.

Part 1: Implement a Simple ETL Pipeline

Step 1: Create an Azure Data Factory Pipeline

1. **Set Up Azure Data Factory (ADF):**
   - In the **Azure Portal**, search for **Azure Data Factory** and create a new instance.
   - Name your instance (e.g., ETL-ADF-Pipeline) and assign it to a resource group.
2. **Ingest Data from Azure Data Lake:**
   - In **ADF Studio**, navigate to **Author** > **Pipelines** and create a new pipeline.
   - Add a **Copy Data** activity to copy raw data from an **Azure Data Lake** storage container to a staging area or directly to Databricks.
   - Configure the source as **Azure Data Lake** and choose your **CSV** file.
   - Set the destination to **Databricks** or **Synapse Analytics**.

Step 2: Create a Databricks Notebook for Data Transformation

1. **Set Up Databricks:**
   - In the Azure Portal, create a **Databricks workspace**.
   - Create a new **cluster** in Databricks with autoscaling enabled to manage resources dynamically.
   - Install any required **libraries** (e.g., pyspark, azure-storage-blob).
2. **Create a Databricks Notebook:**
   - Open the **Databricks workspace** and create a new **Notebook** (e.g., ETL_Transformations).
   - Use the following Spark code to read data from **ADLS**, clean and transform it, and store the results in **Parquet** format.

Databricks Transformation Code:

```
# Import necessary libraries
from pyspark.sql import SparkSession
from pyspark.sql.functions import col

# Create a Spark session
spark = SparkSession.builder.appName("ETL_Pipeline_Optimization").getOrCreate()

# Read raw sales data from Azure Data Lake (CSV format)
raw_data_path = "abfss://<container>@<storage-account>.dfs.core.windows.net/sales_data.csv"
raw_df = spark.read.csv(raw_data_path, header=True, inferSchema=True)

# Data Transformation: Filter invalid data and calculate total sales per region
cleaned_df = raw_df.filter(col("Quantity") > 0).groupBy("Region").agg({"SalesAmount": "sum"})

# Optimize: Write transformed data to Azure Data Lake in Parquet format for efficient storage
optimized_data_path = "abfss://<container>@<storage-account>.dfs.core.windows.net/sales_data_optimized.parquet"
cleaned_df.write.mode("overwrite").parquet(optimized_data_path)
```

3. **Save the Notebook:** This notebook reads data from ADLS, applies a basic transformation, and writes the output to ADLS in **Parquet** format for better performance.

Step 3: Load Data into Azure Synapse Analytics

1. **Set Up Azure Synapse Analytics:**
   - In **Azure Portal**, create an **Azure Synapse Analytics** workspace.
   - Within the Synapse workspace, create a **SQL pool** to store the transformed data.
2. **Modify Databricks Notebook to Load Data:**
   - Update your Databricks Notebook to load the **Parquet** file into **Azure Synapse Analytics**.

Loading Data into Synapse Code:

```
# Define Synapse connection details
synapse_jdbc_url = "jdbc:sqlserver://<synapse-server-name>.database.windows.net:1433;database=<synapse-database>"
username = "<your-username>"
password = "<your-password>"

# Write the cleaned data into Azure Synapse Analytics
cleaned_df.write \
    .format("com.databricks.spark.sqldw") \
    .option("url", synapse_jdbc_url) \
    .option("dbtable", "SalesSummary") \
    .option("user", username) \
    .option("password", password) \
    .mode("overwrite") \
    .save()
```

3. **Run the Notebook:** Execute the notebook to complete the ETL pipeline.

Part 2: Optimize the ETL Pipeline

Step 4: Optimize the Pipeline with Partitioning and Caching

1. **Partition the Data:**
    - Partitioning data improves the performance of distributed processing. In this case, we will partition the data by a commonly queried column such as **Region**.

Partitioning Code:

```
# Partition data by Region for optimized performance
partitioned_df = cleaned_df.repartition("Region")

# Write partitioned data back to Azure Data Lake in Parquet format
partitioned_data_path = "abfss://<container>@<storage-account>.dfs.core.windows.net/sales_data_partitioned.parquet"
partitioned_df.write.mode("overwrite").parquet(partitioned_data_path)
```

2. **Cache Intermediate Results:**
    - Caching intermediate Data Frames helps avoid recomputing the same transformations in later stages of the pipeline.

Caching Code:

```
# Cache the partitioned DataFrame to optimize performance
partitioned_df.cache()

# Perform further transformations or load to Synapse
```

Part 3: Set Up Monitoring in Azure Data Factory

Step 5: Set Up Monitoring and Alerts

1. **Configure Monitoring in ADF:**
   - Go to the **Monitor** tab in **Azure Data Factory**.
   - You will see an overview of all pipeline runs, including their statuses (Success, Failed, In Progress), start times, and durations.
   - Click on a specific pipeline run to drill down into activity-level performance metrics.
2. **Set Up Alerts:**
   - In the **Monitor** tab, click **New Alert Rule** to create a performance-based alert.
   - Example alert condition: If the pipeline execution time exceeds 60 minutes or if any pipeline activity fails.

Example Alert Configuration:

- **Condition:** Execution time > 60 minutes
- **Action Group:** Email notification to the data engineering team
- **Alert Severity:** Critical

This ensures that you are notified immediately if there are any delays or issues with the ETL pipeline.

Part 4: Testing and Validation

Step 6: Run the Optimized ETL Pipeline

1. **Execute the Optimized Pipeline:**
   - In **Azure Data Factory**, trigger the pipeline run.
   - Monitor its execution using the **Monitor** tab to check if the optimizations have reduced the runtime.
2. **Validate Data in Synapse Analytics:**
   - After the pipeline completes, validate that the transformed and optimized data has been successfully loaded into **Azure Synapse Analytics**.

- Run queries on the SalesSummary table to ensure the data has been aggregated and partitioned correctly.

Sample Query to Validate Data in Synapse:

```
SELECT Region, SUM(SalesAmount) AS TotalSales
FROM SalesSummary
GROUP BY Region;
```

Conclusion and Best Practices

In this hands-on assignment, you have successfully implemented a basic ETL pipeline using **Azure Data Factory** and **Databricks**, and optimized it by:

1. Partitioning the data to improve query and processing performance.
2. Using the **Parquet** format to optimize data storage and read performance.
3. Caching intermediate results to minimize redundant computations.
4. Setting up monitoring in Azure Data Factory and configuring alerts to notify you of performance issues.

Assignment Summary:

- Implemented an ETL pipeline that reads data from **Azure Data Lake**, transforms it in **Databricks**, and loads the data into **Azure Synapse Analytics**.
- Optimized the pipeline by partitioning data, caching results, and using the **Parquet** format.
- Set up monitoring and alerting in **Azure Data Factory** to track performance and handle any pipeline issues.

This hands-on exercise lays the foundation for building scalable, efficient, and maintainable ETL pipelines, ensuring that your data infrastructure can handle growing workloads while remaining performant and reliable.

Chapter 8: Data Ethics and Responsible Data Handling

In the age of big data and advanced analytics, the responsible handling of data is more critical than ever. Data ethics refers to the moral and ethical considerations surrounding the collection, storage, processing, and sharing of data. This chapter explores the importance of data ethics, the challenges it presents, and the best practices for ensuring responsible data handling in the field of data engineering.

The Significance of Data Ethics

Data ethics is a topic of increasing importance in the digital age, with numerous implications for businesses, governments, and individuals. The significance of data ethics can be summarized in several key points:

1. **Privacy Concerns**: The collection of vast amounts of personal data has raised concerns about individuals' privacy rights and how their data is being used.
2. **Data Misuse**: Data can be misused for malicious purposes, including identity theft, fraud, and discriminatory practices, underscoring the need for ethical data handling.
3. **Bias and Discrimination**: Data analysis and machine learning models can inadvertently perpetuate biases, leading to discriminatory outcomes, which is a major ethical concern.
4. **Reputation and Trust**: Mishandling data can harm an organization's reputation and erode the trust of customers and stakeholders.

5. **Regulatory Compliance**: Many regions and industries are subject to data protection regulations, such as the GDPR in Europe and HIPAA in healthcare, making ethical data handling a legal requirement.
6. **Transparency and Accountability**: Ethical data practices demand transparency in data collection, processing, and sharing, as well as accountability for any misuse or breaches.

Challenges in Data Ethics

The responsible handling of data presents several challenges in the realm of data engineering:

1. **Data Privacy**: Balancing the collection of data for legitimate purposes with respecting individual privacy rights is a complex challenge.
2. **Data Security**: Ensuring data is kept secure from breaches, cyberattacks, and unauthorized access is an ongoing concern.
3. **Bias Mitigation**: Recognizing and mitigating biases in data and algorithms is critical to avoiding discriminatory outcomes.
4. **Data Sharing**: Determining what data can be shared and under what circumstances, while maintaining data privacy, is a challenging ethical question.
5. **Consent and Transparency**: Obtaining informed consent for data collection and ensuring transparency in data practices can be challenging, especially in a rapidly evolving digital landscape.

Best Practices for Data Ethics

To navigate the challenges of data ethics and ensure responsible data handling, organizations and data professionals should adhere to best practices that promote ethical data use. These best practices include:

1. **Data Governance**: Implement a robust data governance framework that includes data ethics policies and procedures to govern data collection, processing, and sharing.
2. **Data Anonymization**: Anonymize or pseudonymize data whenever possible to protect individual privacy while still enabling data analysis.
3. **Informed Consent**: Obtain informed consent from individuals before collecting their personal data, ensuring they understand how their data will be used.
4. **Data Minimization**: Collect only the data that is necessary for the intended purpose, reducing the risk of misuse.
5. **Data Quality Checks**: Apply data quality checks to identify and address data inaccuracies, reducing the risk of erroneous conclusions and outcomes.
6. **Bias Identification and Mitigation**: Regularly assess data and algorithms for biases and take steps to mitigate bias to prevent discriminatory outcomes.
7. **Data Security Measures**: Implement robust data security measures, including encryption, access controls, and intrusion detection, to protect data from breaches.
8. **Data Transparency**: Be transparent about data collection and use practices, including what data is being collected, for what purpose, and how it will be processed.

9. **Data Retention Policies**: Develop data retention policies to define how long data will be retained and when it will be securely disposed of.
10. **Ethical Data Training**: Provide training to data professionals and stakeholders on the ethical considerations of data handling, including bias awareness and mitigation.

Ethical Considerations in Data Modeling

Data modeling plays a crucial role in data engineering, as it defines how data is structured and used for analysis. Ethical considerations in data modeling include:

1. **Data Bias**: Be aware of potential biases in data that may perpetuate discrimination or unfair practices. Assess and address bias in modeling and analysis.
2. **Data Privacy**: Ensure that data modeling practices respect individuals' privacy by anonymizing or pseudonymizing sensitive data.
3. **Data Transparency**: Make data modeling choices transparent and document the rationale behind decisions to promote accountability.
4. **Data Retention**: Implement data retention policies in data modeling to prevent the unnecessary retention of data and the potential for misuse.

Data Ethics in Real-World Applications

To illustrate the importance of data ethics in real-world scenarios, let's consider a few examples:

1. **Healthcare and Medical Research**: In healthcare, data ethics is crucial for safeguarding patient privacy,

ensuring data security, and avoiding discriminatory practices in medical research. Ethical data handling can lead to improved patient care, more effective treatments, and better health outcomes.

2. **E-commerce and Personalization**: Online retailers use customer data for personalization and recommendation systems. Ethical data practices are essential to protect user privacy, prevent discriminatory pricing, and maintain trust with customers.
3. **Financial Services**: Financial institutions must handle customer data ethically to prevent fraud, protect sensitive financial information, and adhere to strict regulatory requirements. Ethical data practices help maintain the integrity and trustworthiness of the financial system.
4. **Social Media and User Data**: Social media platforms collect vast amounts of user data. Ethical data handling in this context is necessary to protect user privacy, prevent the spread of misinformation, and ensure responsible content moderation.

Conclusion

Data ethics and responsible data handling are fundamental principles in the field of data engineering. As data becomes increasingly central to decision-making, it is crucial to consider the ethical implications of data collection, processing, and sharing.

Organizations and data professionals must prioritize data ethics by implementing best practices, ethical data governance, and transparency in data handling. By doing so, they can build and maintain trust with customers and stakeholders while ensuring compliance with data protection regulations. Responsible data handling is not only an ethical imperative but also a competitive advantage in a world where data-driven decision-making is the norm.

In the following chapters, we will continue to explore key topics in data engineering, including emerging data engineering technologies, the evolving landscape of data analytics, and future trends in data engineering. These topics are essential for building resilient and efficient data systems that empower organizations to make data-driven decisions and unlock new opportunities.

Chapter 9: Real World Case Studies

In this chapter, we will explore real-world scenarios where Data Engineering principles come to life. You will walk through practical implementations of data pipelines using Azure services and Python. Each case study will cover end-to-end pipelines, with insights on best practices for scalability, data quality, and business intelligence. Additionally, we will dive into real code examples and architectural diagrams to give you hands-on experience building data pipelines that solve specific business problems.

Case Study 1: Building a Scalable Data Pipeline

Scenario:

A retail company needs to process sales data from millions of transactions every day. They need a scalable data pipeline that ingests, processes, and stores data in a data warehouse, enabling real-time analytics and reporting.

Architecture Overview:

1. Data Ingestion: Raw sales data from multiple sources (API, CSV files) is ingested into Azure Data Lake Storage (ADLS).

2. Data Processing: Data is cleaned, transformed, and prepared for analysis using Azure Databricks.

3. Data Storage: Processed data is loaded into an Azure Synapse data warehouse.

4. Reporting: Data is visualized and analyzed using Power BI.

Diagram:

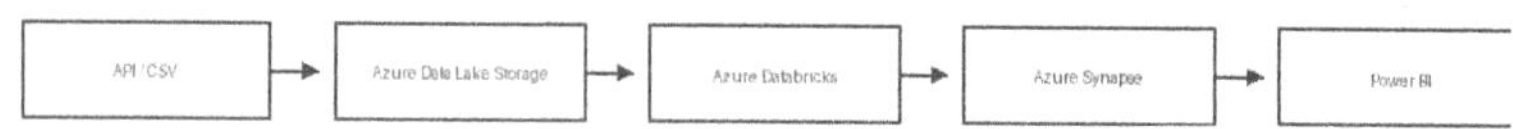

Step-by-Step Solution:

1. **Ingest Data into ADLS:** Ingest raw data from multiple sources into Azure Data Lake using Azure Data Factory.

```
from azure.storage.blob import BlobServiceClient

blob_service_client = BlobServiceClient.from_connection_string("your_connection_string")
container_client = blob_service_client.get_container_client("sales-data")

# Upload CSV file
with open("sales_data.csv", "rb") as data:
    container_client.upload_blob(name="raw/sales_data.csv", data=data)
```

2. **Transform Data in Databricks:** Use Databricks to transform raw data and prepare it for analytics.

```
from pyspark.sql import SparkSession

spark = SparkSession.builder.appName("SalesDataProcessing").getOrCreate()
df = spark.read.csv("/mnt/sales_data/raw/sales_data.csv", header=True, inferSchema=True)

# Transformations
df = df.withColumn("total_sales", df["quantity_sold"] * df["unit_price"])

# Write to ADLS
df.write.format("parquet").save("/mnt/sales_data/processed/sales_data.parquet")
```

3. **Load Data into Azure Synapse:** Use Azure Synapse to create a relational data warehouse and load the processed data.

```
CREATE TABLE SalesData (
    TransactionID INT,
    ProductID INT,
    QuantitySold INT,
    TotalSales FLOAT
);

COPY INTO SalesData
FROM 'https://<your_adls_url>/processed/sales_data.parquet'
WITH (
    FILE_FORMAT = 'Parquet',
    IDENTITY_INSERT = 'ON'
);
```

4. **Visualize Data with Power BI:** Connect Power BI to Azure Synapse to create dashboards for sales data insights.

- **Dashboard Example:** A sales performance dashboard that tracks total sales, best-selling products, and revenue trends.

Case Study 2: Data Quality Assurance in Practice

Scenario:

A financial institution needs to implement a quality assurance system for incoming loan application data. The system must ensure data accuracy and compliance with regulatory standards before it is loaded into their data warehouse.

Architecture Overview:

1. Data Ingestion: Loan applications are ingested into Azure Data Lake.
2. Data Quality Checks: Azure Databricks performs quality checks such as missing value handling, duplicate detection, and range validation.
3. Data Storage: Cleaned data is stored in Azure Synapse.

Diagram:

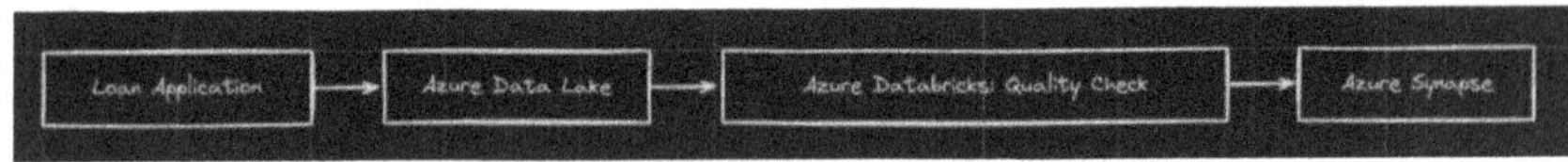

Step-by-Step Solution:

1. **Ingest Data into ADLS:** Ingest loan application data into Azure Data Lake using Azure Data Factory.

```
# Blob service connection code (same as Case Study 1)
```

```
from azure.storage.blob import BlobServiceClient

blob_service_client = BlobServiceClient.from_connection_string("your_connection_string")
container_client = blob_service_client.get_container_client("sales-data")

# Upload CSV file
with open("sales_data.csv", "rb") as data:
    container_client.upload_blob(name="raw/sales_data.csv", data=data)
```

2. **Perform Data Quality Checks in Databricks:**

```
from pyspark.sql.functions import col

df = spark.read.csv("/mnt/loan_applications/raw/applications.csv", header=True, inferSchema=True)

# Data Quality Checks
df_clean = df.filter(df['loan_amount'].isNotNull())  # Remove rows with null loan amounts
df_clean = df_clean.dropDuplicates(['application_id'])  # Remove duplicate applications

# Write clean data to ADLS
df_clean.write.format("parquet").save("/mnt/loan_applications/cleaned/applications.parquet")
```

3. Load Data into Azure Synapse:

```
CREATE TABLE LoanApplications (
    ApplicationID INT,
    CustomerID INT,
    LoanAmount FLOAT
);

COPY INTO LoanApplications
FROM 'https://<your_adls_url>/cleaned/applications.parquet'
WITH (
    FILE_FORMAT = 'Parquet',
    IDENTITY_INSERT = 'ON'
);
```

4. **Data Governance and Reporting:** Use Azure Purview to track data lineage and ensure compliance with regulations. Reports are generated for audit purposes using Power BI.

Case Study 3: Data Engineering for Business Intelligence

Scenario:

A multinational company wants to build a business intelligence pipeline that combines sales data from multiple regions into a centralized data warehouse for real-time analytics and reporting.

Architecture Overview:

1. Data Ingestion: Ingest sales data from different regions into ADLS.
2. Data Transformation: Use Databricks for cleaning, aggregating, and unifying the data.
3. Data Storage: Store the unified data in Azure Synapse.
4. Business Intelligence: Use Power BI to generate dashboards for regional sales performance.

Diagram:

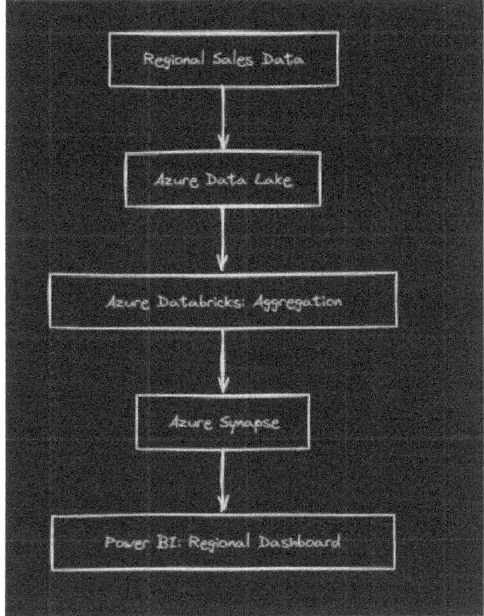

Step-by-Step Solution:

1. **Ingest Data into ADLS:** Ingest sales data from different regions into Azure Data Lake Storage.

Blob service connection code (same as Case Study 1)

```
from azure.storage.blob import BlobServiceClient

blob_service_client = BlobServiceClient.from_connection_string("your_connection_string")
container_client = blob_service_client.get_container_client("sales-data")

# Upload CSV file
with open("sales_data.csv", "rb") as data:
    container_client.upload_blob(name="raw/sales_data.csv", data=data)
```

2. Transform and Aggregate Data in Databricks:

```
df_north = spark.read.csv("/mnt/sales_data/north/region.csv", header=True, inferSchema=True)
df_south = spark.read.csv("/mnt/sales_data/south/region.csv", header=True, inferSchema=True)

# Combine data
df_combined = df_north.union(df_south)

# Aggregation
df_aggregated = df_combined.groupBy("region").agg({"sales": "sum"}).withColumnRenamed("sum(sales)", "total_sales")

# Write to ADLS
df_aggregated.write.format("parquet").save("/mnt/sales_data/aggregated/total_sales.parquet")
```

3. Load Data into Azure Synapse:

```
CREATE TABLE RegionalSales (
    Region VARCHAR(50),
    TotalSales FLOAT
);

COPY INTO RegionalSales
FROM 'https://<your_adls_url>/aggregated/total_sales.parquet'
WITH (
    FILE_FORMAT = 'Parquet',
    IDENTITY_INSERT = 'ON'
);
```

Visualize Data with Power BI: Create a sales dashboard that shows regional sales performance with drill-down features for further analysis.

Bonus Use Case: ETL with Azure ADF using ADLS & AML services

Detailed Technical Architecture

The below figure shows high-level current state architecture diagram.

1. Input zip folder with SFTP is received in the ADLS Blob Storage (rawzipped)

2. ADF pipeline Zip's the file extracts from Blob to respective folders in Blob Storage (rawunzipped)

3. ADF executes the Azure ML Pipeline using Python wrappers.

4. Python wrappers will clean and process the dashboard input files and then push them back to ADLS Blob storage (validate).

5. Python code will write the final data into 2 different folders as per their output type or data contains. For example, for drop and load type data it will write the csv files into FinalOutput folder whereas for append data it will write data into FinalOutputAppend Folder

6. ADF pipeline will copy data from CSV files and push them into the Database.

7. Final data published into SharePoint as well which is used as input data to Power BI.

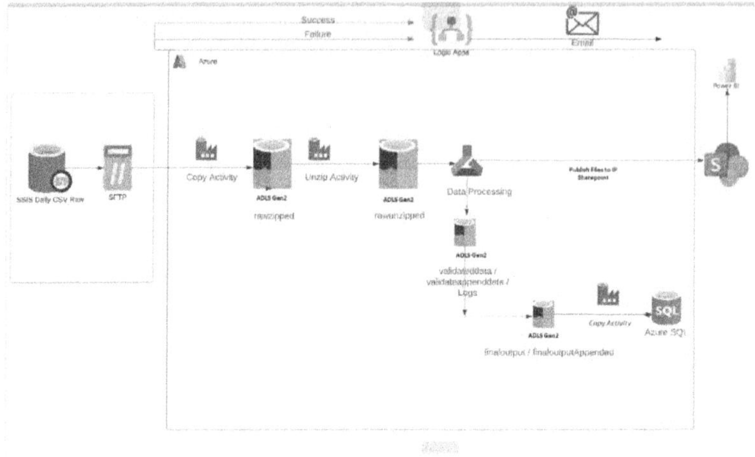

1)Azure Data Lake Storage (ADLS): Azure Data Lake is built on Azure Blob storage designed to store, process, and secure large amounts of structured, semi-structured, and unstructured data

2)Azure Data Factory: It is a cloud-based ETL and data integration service that allows you to create data-driven workflows for orchestrating data movement and transforming data at scale.

3)Azure Logic Apps: Email Triggering mechanism regarding the workflow status

4)Azure Machine Learning: It provides the environment to run all the Python wrappers for data cleansing and other transformations.

ADF Master Pipeline

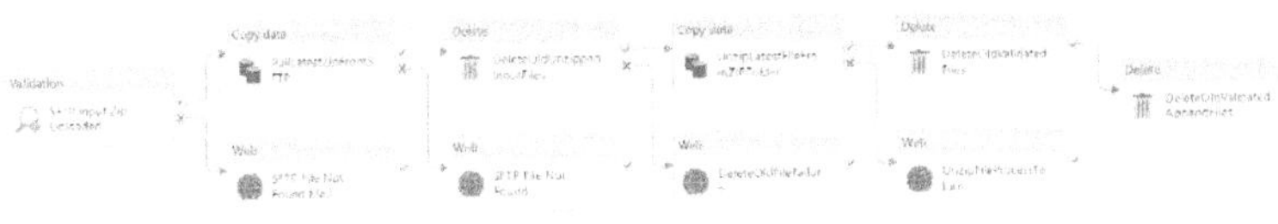

(Copy activity by SFTP to ADLS)

(ETL Process and Copy Activity to Store data into DB)

Closing Thoughts from my side:

As we reach the end of this journey through **Data Engineering: A Practical Approach**, I want to take a moment to reflect on the transformative role that data engineering plays in today's world. Throughout this book, we've explored the essential concepts and techniques that power data-driven organizations—from building scalable ETL pipelines and designing efficient data warehouses to ensuring data quality, governance, and security. These are not just theoretical constructs, but the very foundation upon which modern enterprises thrive.

By following along with the hands-on exercises and applying real-world examples, you now possess the skills to navigate the complex data landscape. You've learned how to:

- **Architect and implement scalable data pipelines** using tools like **Azure Data Factory** and **Databricks**.
- **Optimize data storage and processing** using techniques like partitioning, caching, and leveraging efficient formats like **Parquet**.
- **Ensure data quality and governance** through data lineage tracking, profiling, and implementing robust governance frameworks with **Azure Purview**.
- **Secure your data** while maintaining compliance with regulatory standards by applying encryption, access control, and monitoring best practices.

These skills are invaluable not just for today, but for the future, as the demand for data-driven solutions continues to grow. Data engineers are at the forefront of this revolution, building the infrastructure that powers everything from business analytics to machine learning models.

What's Next?

The world of data engineering is vast and ever-evolving. New tools, techniques, and challenges will continue to emerge as technology advances and data becomes even more integral to decision-making. But remember, the principles you've learned here—whether it's the fundamentals of data modeling, the importance of data quality, or the power of scalable data pipelines—will remain the cornerstones of effective data engineering for years to come.

I encourage you to continue exploring, experimenting, and refining your skills. Whether you're applying these concepts to real-world projects, collaborating with data scientists, or optimizing enterprise systems, always strive for efficiency, accuracy, and reliability in your data solutions.

A Final Word

As an author, my goal was to provide a comprehensive, practical guide to help you not only understand the theory but also apply it in real-world scenarios. If you've made it to this point, you're well on your way to becoming a proficient data engineer. But remember, learning is a continuous process—there's always more to discover and new challenges to solve.

As you move forward in your data engineering journey, don't hesitate to revisit the concepts covered in this book. Whether you're designing a new pipeline, troubleshooting performance issues, or ensuring regulatory compliance, these chapters are meant to serve as a resource you can return to, time and time again.

Thank you for taking the time to immerse yourself in this material. I hope it has been as rewarding for you to read as it was for me to write. The data engineering field is filled with opportunity and innovation, and I'm excited to see how you will contribute to it.

Stay Connected

I'd love to hear about your experiences, challenges, and successes as you apply what you've learned from this book. Feel free to reach out or connect with me on platforms like **LinkedIn**, where we can continue to discuss and explore the evolving field of data engineering.

Here's to your continued success in the world of data engineering—may your pipelines always run efficiently, your data always be clean, and your systems always be scalable.

Achieved *Amazon Best Seller* status in two competitive categories for the book *Mastering Generative AI: From Langchain to Real-World Applications*.

Best regards,
Sandeep Kumar Pandey
Azure Architect, Technology Enthusiast and Financial Educator.

[Certified FPMP, (Financial Planning & Mentorship Program)].

www.ingramcontent.com/pod-product-compliance
Ingram Content Group UK Ltd.
Pitfield, Milton Keynes, MK11 3LW, UK
UKHW022019190726
13853UKWH00005B/2008

9 798895 447284